FOUL DEEDS AND SUSPICIOUS DEATHS IN LEEDS

'FOUL DEEDS AND SUSPICIOUS DEATHS' Series

Foul Deeds and Suspicious Deaths series explores in detail crimes of passion, brutal murders, grisly deeds and foul misdemeanours. From Victorian street crime, to more modern murder where passion, jealousy, or social depravation brought unexpected violence to those involved. From mysterious death to murder and manslaughter, the books are a fascinating insight into not only those whose lives are forever captured by the suffering they endured, but also into the society that moulded and shaped their lives. Each book takes you on a journey into the darker and unknown side of the area.

Other titles in the series

Foul Deeds and Suspicious Deaths in Blackburn & Hyndburn, Stephen Greenhalgh
1 903425 18 2 • £9.99

Foul Deeds & Suspicious Deaths In and Around Chesterfield, Geoffrey Sadler
1 903425 30 1 • £9.99

Foul Deeds and Suspicious Deaths In and Around Durham, Maureen Anderson
1 903425 46 8, £9.99

Foul Deeds and Suspicious Deaths in Nottingham, Kevin Turton
1 903425 35 2 • £9.99

Foul Deeds & Suspicious Deaths In and Around Rotherham, Kevin Turton
1 903425 27 1 • £9.99

Foul Deeds & Suspicious Deaths In and Around The Tees, Maureen Anderson
1 903425 26 3 • £9.99

Foul Deeds & Suspicious Deaths in Wakefield, Kate Taylor
1 903425 07 7 • £9.99

More Foul Deeds and Suspicious Deaths in Wakefield, Kate Taylor
1 903425 48 4 • £9.99

Foul Deeds & Suspicious Deaths in York, Keith Henson
1 903425 33 6 • £9.99

Foul Deeds & Suspicious Deaths on the Yorkshire Coast, Alan Whitworth
1 903425 01 8 • £9.99

Other West Yorkshire titles

Aspects of Bradford, Bob Duckett • 1 871647 55 X • £9.95
Aspects of Bradford 2, Bob Duckett • 1 871647 82 7 • £9.95
Aspects of Calderdale, John Billingsley • 1 903425 20 4 • £9.99
Aspects of Huddersfield, Isobel Schofield • 1 871647 66 5 • £9.95
Aspects of Huddersfield 2, Stephen Wade • 1 903425 23 9 • £9.99
Aspects of Leeds 2, Lynne Stevenson Tate • 1 871647 59 2 • £9.95
Aspects of Leeds 3, Lynne Stevenson Tate • 1 903425 05 0 • £9.99
Aspects of Wakefield 2, Kate Taylor • 1 871647 68 1 • £9.95
Aspects of Wakefield 3, Kate Taylor • 1 903425 06 9 • £9.95
Boxing in Leeds & Bradford, Ronnie Wharton • 1 903425 10 7 • £9.99
Canals & River Section of the Aire & Calder Navigation
Mike Taylor • 1 903425 37 9 • £9.99
From Wakefield to Towton, Philip Haigh • 0 85052 825 9 • £9.95
Leeds Pals, Laurie Milner • 0 85052 335 4 • £17.95
Making of the West Yorkshire Landscape, Anthony Silson • 1 903425 31 X • £9.99
The Making of Huddersfield, George Redmonds • 1 903425 39 5 • £9.99
Trams Around Dewsbury & Wakefield, Norman Ellis • 1 903425 40 9 • £9.99

Please contact us via any of the methods below for more information or a catalogue.

WHARNCLIFFE BOOKS
47 Church Street • Barnsley • South Yorkshire • S70 2AS

Tel: 01226 734555 • 734222   Fax: 01226 734438
E-mail: enquiries@pen-and-sword.co.uk • **Website:** www.wharncliffebooks.co.uk

Foul Deeds & Suspicious Deaths In
LEEDS

DAVID GOODMAN

Series Editor
Brian Elliott

Wharncliffe Books

First Published in 2003 by
Wharncliffe Books
an imprint of
Pen and Sword Books Limited,
47 Church Street, Barnsley,
South Yorkshire. S70 2AS

Copyright © David Goodman 2003

For up-to-date information on other titles produced under the
Wharncliffe imprint, please telephone or write to:

> **Wharncliffe Books**
> **FREEPOST**
> **47 Church Street**
> **Barnsley**
> **South Yorkshire S70 2BR**
> **Telephone (24 hours): 01226 734555**

ISBN: 1-903425-08-5

A CIP catalogue record of this book is available from the
British Library

Cover illustration: *Front –* Marsh Lane Police Station. *Leeds Library and Information Services*
Rear – The grave of Barbara Waterhouse in Horsforth Cemetery. *The author*

Printed in the United Kingdom by
CPI UK

Contents

Introduction

When first approached by Wharncliffe Books about writing *Foul Deeds and Suspicious Deaths in Leeds* I was somewhat reluctant. It is not the most pleasant topic on which to write, even though there is now considerable distance between the crimes and the present day. However, I need not have worried. It has been a fascinating venture and I only hope I have done justice to it.

The book features many of the murders, which shocked Leeds during Victorian times. Many people with an interest in local history will have heard of Charlie Peace, one of the most notorious murderers of the nineteenth century. Also, Mary Bateman's name was known outside of Leeds through the nature of the crime and being known as the 'Yorkshire Witch'. However, there are many other stories in the book, which have been largely forgotten for over one hundred years. Whether it be Louie Calvert, known as the Boot Fetishist, William Dove who slowly poisoned his wife to death or Thomas Mellor who drowned his daughters in the Leeds/Liverpool Canal, they are all interesting stories which deserve re-telling.

Part of my interest in the research for this book was in looking beyond the bare facts of each individual case. William Dove killing his wife is not, in itself, particularly interesting. However, it was the method behind his crime, what drove him to commit such an act and how he was detected that makes this case and others so compelling. I have also tried to convey, in some small way, the conditions in which people lived during the nineteenth and early twentieth century. Many of the victims and murderers featured lived in poverty and this makes an interesting backdrop to the stories.

There are many people who have helped me in the researching and writing of this book. Firstly Brian Elliott, Rachael Wilkinson and all at Wharncliffe Books who have always been available and willing to give advice and support when needed. The staff at the local studies libraries in Leeds, Bradford and Batley have also been very helpful during the long hours of research. Apologies to the poor people sat next to me at the microfilm machines who heard me dictate, in a sinister whisper, the most fearsome details. I hope I didn't give you nightmares!

The Horsforth Village Museum Society was extremely helpful with regard to the Barbara Waterhouse case, providing photographs as well as supplementary information and I am very grateful to the staff at the museum.

The majority of the photographs and cartoons of Armley Prison are being held at the West Yorkshire Archive Service in Wakefield. However, permission to use them had to be given by Armley and I have Richard Branch, Human Resources Manager at the prison to thank for the fact that they are featured in the book. Also Ruth Harris at Wakefield Archives deserves my thanks for her help with the matter. Colleagues and other staff at West Yorkshire Archive Service have always been helpful when I have asked for advice and I am very grateful.

Alan Humphries at the Thackray Medical Museum was also a great help when I was researching the Mary Bateman case and the resurrectionists, as were the staff at York Castle Museum archives.

Finally, a huge thank you to my wife Julie. When I suggested a family outing last New Year's Day she probably did not imagine that we would be taking photographs of graveyards and other sites in Leeds with links to one or more of the murders. Did she complain? Well, frankly yes she did, but she has been a huge support in every way, often making phone calls on my behalf when I pretended to be too busy. She was also a rather too critical proofreader of a couple of the chapters!

I do hope you enjoy reading *Foul Deeds and Suspicious Deaths in Leeds*. I can honestly say that, despite the gruesome nature of the crimes involved, it has been a huge pleasure and privilege to write.

Chapter 1

Influenced by a Wizard
1856

Harriet Dove's death in 1856 was a puzzle to the surgeons who had come to know her in the weeks leading to her death. A complaint that affected her stomach and nervous system increased in intensity until she eventually died in agony. However, what caused her death? Her grieving husband gave no hint as to his part in her death, but sharp-eyed detectives soon saw evidence leading directly to William Dove.

William Dove's parents, Christopher and Mary, hailed from Darlington but moved to Leeds and built up a successful leather business. Their son, Christopher Junior was planning to enter the family business but fell ill with tuberculosis and he died in 1836, aged sixteen, becoming the first person to be buried in Oxford Place. Exactly twenty years later, at York Castle, Christopher's brother William would die at the hands of a hangman.

William did not show the same aptitude for business as his brother, failing at school and college before briefly emigrating to America. On his return to Britain he settled in Leeds and eventually met Harriet Jenkins. The couple married in 1852 but it was a desperately unhappy marriage. Dove was twenty-eight years of age, thin, middle-sized and respectable looking. However, he was a heavy drinker and possessed a violent temper. On 22 August 1854 he was taken into custody on a charge of threatening to shoot his father and attempting 'self-destruction'. There were moments when William was kind and thoughtful to his wife but they became less frequent as time wore on and his behaviour deteriorated into brutal and violent outbursts, usually drink-related. In addition, Harriet was often ill and her costly medical bills infuriated her husband.

He became so violent towards her that Harriet grew concerned about her welfare. She told her servant, Elizabeth

Fisher, that in the event of her death, she should call on friends to insist upon a post-mortem, as she was worried that foul play might be the cause.

In the meantime William Dove had met a man called Henry Harrison who described himself as a wizard. Impressed by Harrison's alleged gifts, Dove allowed the 'wizard' to influence him in all his decisions, including the thorny problem of his relationship with his wife. Harrison preyed on Dove's own doubts about his marriage, saying that he would never be happy until his wife was dead. Dove asked Harrison to put a spell onto his wife so that the two of them could live happily together.

However, this did not work and thoughts began to turn to how Dove could rid himself of Harriet. One day Dove was in Harrison's warehouse, opposite his home when the 'wizard' told him that belladonna could not be found in the human body after death, especially if it was in a crystallised state.

In 1856 William Dove became obsessed with the case of the

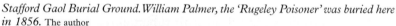

Stafford Gaol Burial Ground. William Palmer, the 'Rugeley Poisoner' was buried here in 1856. The author

notorious Staffordshire poisoner William Palmer who had made the headlines with his crimes. Palmer set up practice as a GP in Staffordshire. However, through gambling he acquired large debts and as his debts increased, members of his family began to die off in mysterious circumstances. He killed his mother-in-law, then his wife, brother, four of his children and several of his known creditors.

Palmer finally came unstuck after killing a friend he had gone racing with. The man's wealthy family demanded an autopsy at which poison was found and Palmer was accused of murder. He was found guilty, and on 14 June 1856 he was hanged at Stafford jail in front of more than 50,000 onlookers.

Dove read that strychnine was one of the poisons used and it was extremely difficult to detect. With this in mind he went to the doctor's to see if this was true. On 10 February 1856, Dove told the doctor's assistant that his neighbourhood was blighted with cats and mice and he wanted some poison to get rid of them. Elletson, the doctor's assistant gave ten grains of strychnine to Dove who experimented with it by killing a cat. He returned to the surgery and had claimed that rain had washed all the poison away. Elletson provided Dove with five more grains.

The ever-watchful eye of Elizabeth Fisher kept William Dove in check. However, the opportunity Dove was looking for came in February 1856 when Elizabeth Fisher was taken ill and could no longer care for Harriet Dove. She sent her mother to care for Harriet, but during these few days, Harriet Dove's condition began to deteriorate.

Dr Morley, who had been treating her for a stomach disorder and problems with her nervous system, was puzzled by the new problems and prescribed her some strong dark, anti-spasmodic medicine. Her husband took a cork out of one of the bottles of medicine and touched the wet end of it with the drug. He then replaced the cork and shook up the bottle. He had also put a small quantity of strychnine in some jelly that his sister had made and which his wife tasted. Over the next four days Harriet grew worse with increased twitches and convulsions. However, she was grateful that her dutiful husband appeared to care for her. She said: 'Whenever it is time to have any medicine, Mr

SERIOUS CHARGE OF
SLOW POISONING
WITH
STRYCHNINE,
AT LEEDS.
THE ADJOURNED INQUEST,
YESTERDAY.

The adjourned inquest on the body of Harriet Dove, aged 28, wife of Mr. William Dove, Cardigan Place, Burley, near Leeds, was held yesterday at the Leeds Court House, before Mr. Blackburn, borough coroner, and the jury before whom the previous inquiries have been held. The evidence was of an important character, but in justice to Mr. Dove, who is in custody, charged with poisoning the deceased, we abstain from comments, referring our readers to the evidence itself, as given below.

As stated in the *Intelligencer* on Saturday the prisoner is the son of the late Mr. Christopher Dove, currier, Callane. After leaving school he was, we understand, placed with a respectable farmer in the neighbourhood of Scarbro' and subsequently he took a farm near Bramham. About three years and a half ago, he married the deceased, who was the daughter of a respectable yeoman lately residing near Plymouth, (not Bramhope as stated on Saturday), but now dead, and sister to Mr. Jenkins, professor of mathematics at Madras. Subsequently they went to reside at Woodhouse, near Normanton, and in November last they came to reside at Cardigan-place. Mrs. Jenkins and a daughter came to Leeds yesterday week, on a visit to the deceased, not having heard of her death, prior to leaving Plymouth. The prisoner, who is a thin, middle-sized, respectable looking man, is twenty-eight years of age, and has for some years been addicted to habits of intemperance. He appears to have been of a somewhat violent temper, and on the 22nd of August, 1854, he was taken into custody on a charge of threatening to shoot his father, and attempting self-destruction. He is very respectably connected, and has been living on an annuity left him by his father. The marriage proved in many respects an unhappy one, and the prisoner's conduct towards the deceased (whom he had frequently threatened to put out of the way) has at times been so violent as to excite doubts as to his sanity, and it will be observed from the evidence below that so serious was the impression upon her own mind that she requested her servant, in the event of her death, to urge her friends to insist upon a *post mortem* examination, as she feared foul play. It is also stated that a short time ago a deed of separation was prepared. They had no family, but it will be seen from the evidence of Mr. Morley that the deceased was *enciente* at the time of her death.

Headline on the inquest into the body of Harriet Dove. Leeds Intelligencer

Dove is always ready by day or night to give it to me.'

Dove continued to put strychnine onto the cork on subsequent days until his wife became seriously ill. On the evening of 1 March 1856 William Dove gave Harriet a dose of the medicine and carefully washed out the glass afterwards in the company of Jane Whitham, a neighbour and Mary Wood, an old servant of the family. Harriet complained of the taste saying: 'oh dear, this is very disagreeable and very hot'. She asked Jane Whitham for a lozenge to take the taste away, but half an hour later she was in agony. Her back was arched and her eyes protruding. William went for medical aid but by the time Dr Morley arrived Harriet was dead. She was buried in an unmarked grave at Beckett Street cemetery.

Dove immediately sought the advice of his mentor Henry Harrison. The 'wizard' asked Dove if he had poisoned his wife, which Dove strenuously denied. Concerned about his fate, Dove asked Harrison whether he would be found out and if he would have to go to prison. Harrison replied that it would be very difficult adding: 'but I can work you out'.

Dove began to become resigned to his fate when a post-mortem was ordered within twenty-four hours of the death, as he had been under the impression that strychnine could not be detected in the body after that time had elapsed. As he expected, the post-mortem revealed that Harriet Dove had been poisoned and the next day Dove was arrested and accused of killing her.

The contents of her stomach were given to two rabbits, two mice and one guinea pig. They all died with similar symptoms. Also, a cleaning lady saw a spaniel drink a quantity of blood from the floor where the post-mortem had been carried out and it died soon afterwards, carrying the symptoms of strychnine.

Part of Dove's statement after his arrest read:

On Thursday, the 6th March, I went to the New Cross Inn and after being there a few minutes I sent for Harrison. He came. I gave him a card announcing my wife's death, at the same time informing him that an inquest was held as to my wife's death. He inquired the reason why the inquest was held. I said my wife died very suddenly and Mr Morley, the surgeon, cannot account for it and it was known that I had strychnine in the house. Mr Morley thinks some might have been spilt, and my wife have got some accidentally. I then said to him 'you told me that strychnine could not be detected, but I have since seen in the Materia Medica *that it can. What is your opinion now?' Professor Taylor said that it cannot be detected twenty-four hours after death in the human body.*

The coroner's inquest relating to the death of Mrs Dove heard Dr Morley, the surgeon, speak of a conversation he had with Mr Dove on the Thursday before his wife died. Dove had wanted to know what Morley had found to be the cause of death, but Morley told him:

We have not yet finished our analysis and I cannot give an opinion, but I cannot say we have not found any natural disease to account for death.

Dove then asked Morley whether the surgeon suspected him of poisoning his wife and whether he thought he could be so cruel.

As she was present during the last days of Harriet Dove's life, Ann Fisher, mother of Elizabeth, gave evidence and said of Harriet's final hours:

Her legs became stiff, there were twitchings of the legs and arm, her body was thrown back; there was the arching back and all the symptoms to which I have called your attention as being produced by strychnine.

The inquest resulted in a verdict of 'wilful murder against William Dove' and he was committed on the coroner's warrant for trial at the summer Assizes for the county.

In July 1856, Dove appeared before Judge Baron Branwell,

accused of poisoning his wife with strychnine. Bertie Markland, for the prosecution, opened by stating:

Gentlemen, this is one of the most cold blooded and cruel murders almost known in the history of crime.

In his defence Dove blamed Henry Harrison for the murder, insisting that he would not have used that or any other poison if it had not been for Harrison who kept on telling him that he would not find happiness until his wife was 'out of the way'. He added:

He then offered to make me some but I declined. I had no desire, at this time, to get rid of my wife. My belief was that Harrison was possessed of some supernatural power, and that he could through some influence compel her to live happily with me... I asked him in February if he could do anything to get her out of the way and he said he would lay her on a sick bed and she would never get better.

I was muddled before this, and didn't know what I was doing. When the thoughts of her death crossed my mind, I immediately regretted what I had done, and I believe if Mr Morley had come in at that moment I should have told him what I had given her, so that he might have used means to restore her. I cannot describe the anguish that I felt when I returned from Mr Morley's and found my wife dead.

The jury returned a verdict of guilty, but they expressed concern about the mental state of William Dove. The Judge forwarded the request for leniency, but stated that he disagreed with it and sentenced Dove to death by hanging, adding:

He wilfully and wickedly destroyed the life of one whom he had solemnly vowed to love and cherish and it appears to us, as it does to ninety-nine out of every hundred of our fellow countrymen who are acquainted with the circumstances of the case, that his life has been justly forfeited – forfeited in accordance with the offended laws of God and man.

On 7 August 1856, Dove's full admission was published in the *Leeds Mercury*. He stated:

On the Saturday after Elizabeth Fisher left, I took the paper containing the strychnine out of the razor case and put it in my waistcoat pocket. I then went to my mother's house. In the afternoon I had previously called at Dr Morley's for my wife's medicine. It was an effervescing draught in two bottles. At my mother's that evening I took the cork out of one of the bottles and touched the wet end of it with strychnine. I then put the cork in the bottle again and shook up the draught...

Later he added:

About three o'clock in the afternoon I went into the stable and took about a grain of strychnine out of the paper and put it in another paper, which I placed into the wine glass which contained a little water... I poured the mixture [her medicine] *into that wine glass... When I saw my wife suffering from the attack on the Saturday night, it flashed across my mind that I had given her the strychnine and she would die from the effects!*

York Castle where William Dove was executed in August 1856. York Castle Museum

Dove spent his final days in a cell in York Castle. He was rational and well aware of what was happening to him. He had confessed his guilt and now awaited his sentence. To pass the time he had regular visits from his family including his mother, two sisters and brother-in-law and also spent much of his time talking to Mr Wright, the prison philanthropist. He freely admitted to Mr Wright that he had poisoned his wife, and that he deserved to die. On the Thursday before his execution Dove also gave a confession of guilt to his solicitor, Mr Barret. The High Sheriff had assured Dove that no cast would be made from his head and he was also assured that no articles belonging to him would leave the Castle.

The *Leeds Intelligencer* gave an insight into Dove's state of mind during his final days:

> *That Dove is fully impressed with the enormity of his crime there is now little doubt, and we were assured by the Rev. Mr Hartley, just before despatching a parcel, that the convict is fully alive to his dreadful position, and is in a truly penitent state of mind. His agony of mind is spoken of as intense, and we are informed that he is so excited as to the fearful doom which awaits him, as to raise fears that the confidence and self-control which has hitherto characterised him will fail him at the last moment. Should this not be the case, some anticipate he will address the crowd.*

In a final letter to his solicitor Mr Barret, Dove once again blamed Harrison for the crime he had committed. He wrote:

> *I would wish to remark that I committed the crime through the instigation of that bad man Henry Harrison, of the South Market, Leeds. Had it not been for him I never should have been in these circumstances.*

News of the death sentence hanging over the head of William Dove captured the imagination of the Leeds public as a case which had them transfixed came to a conclusion. Such was the excitement that scores of people went to see his coffin being made, and his 'rope' went on a tour of local pubs.

Saturday, 9 August 1856, the day of Dove's execution began with a gloomy sky as the workmen finished constructing the scaffold, which had been used on previous occasions and had

The condemned cell at York Castle as it was in the nineteenth century. The author

been examined and repaired the previous day. Crowds stopped throughout the Friday to watch the construction process until it was complete, at about 8 o'clock in the evening. It was placed in the usual position, in the governor's garden. As early as 7 o'clock on the Saturday morning a crowd of about 100 were situated behind the iron railing at St George's Field, in front of the drop, to witness the execution.

By half-past eleven the crowd had grown considerably and by noon there was a crowd of about 20,000. At seven minutes before twelve Dove was transferred to a room in which he was prepared for his final, short journey to the gallows. His solicitor, Mr Barret, asked Dove if there was anything in the statement that he had given two days before that he wished to correct. Dove replied: 'Not a word: it is strictly true'. He then told his solicitor: 'Mr Barret, tell my poor mother I die happy.' They were the last words William Dove spoke, as within seconds, the clock struck noon and the execution procession was formed with the Reverend Hartley and Mr Wright appearing on the scaffold with Dove.

Being placed under the drop, the executioner adjusted the rope, covered Dove's face with a cap and fastened his legs with a cord. The executioner then went up the steps and, drawing the bolt, the drop fell. Death was not instantaneous, Dove struggled violently for some time until his body became still. When the body had been suspended for an hour, it was cut down and was interred the same evening within the precincts of the prison.

Dove's former mentor Henry Harrison did not receive any punishment for his part in the murder of Harriet Dove, but he was later to be prosecuted on three charges of deception and rape. He was sentenced to nine months hard labour for these crimes, but was later also charged with bigamy and received four years in prison.

The Case of the Boot Fetishist
1926

Louie Calvert, a double murderer who became known as the boot fetishist, was one of very few women executed in Britain in the twentieth century. She was found guilty of the murder of Lily Waterhouse, a forty-one-year-old widow, who lived in the New Wortley area of Leeds and, it emerged after her execution, that Calvert had also killed a man called John Frobisher four years earlier.

Louie Gomersal was born at Gawthorpe, near Ossett but in her teens moved to Leeds and worked as a maid for John Frobisher who lived in Mercy Street, Wellington Lane in Leeds, using the name Louisa Jackson.

Frobisher was found floating in a local canal on 12 July 1922 but after his death, Gomersal continued for six months to be a tenant of the house in Mercy Street and took in lodgers from time to time. However, she was forced to leave the house towards the end of 1922, due to non-payment of rent and drifted between jobs until the time she married 'Arty' Calvert at Hunslet Registry Office in August 1925. Louie had an affair with Arthur who was from the Pottery Fields area of Leeds and falsely claimed that she was pregnant by him; forcing him into marriage.

When married, Calvert was aged twenty-nine and had begun work as a weaver. At this time she was quite a regular attender of meetings at the Salvation Army, an organisation which said that everything possible was done to 'bring the woman to the right way of thinking'. However, she continued to display 'wayward habits' and even the army bonnet that she wore was stolen from another member of the organisation.

Calvert had been in trouble with the police during her time with the Salvation Army and one woman, who attended meetings at the same time as Calvert said:

There was always something mysterious about her. At times she

Glasshouse Street as it is today. Louie Calvert married Arthur at Hunslet Registry Office here in August 1925. The author

would break into the filthiest language, and I forbade her on this account to come into my house. She showed a very wicked temper at that, and tried to strike me with a poker, and I think myself lucky to escape as I did. It came to our knowledge that she had several aliases. Louisa Jackson and Edith Thompson were two of them.

At the beginning of March 1926, Louie placed an advert in a local newspaper appealing for a baby to adopt. A teenage girl from Pontefract called Ward replied to the advert. She had an unwanted baby daughter and the two women met up at Leeds railway station when the baby was handed over to Calvert.

Louie did not tell Arthur about the child, but instead continued with the lie that she was pregnant. On Saturday, 8 March, Calvert showed him a letter, written in pencil, which she said was from her sister in Dewsbury inviting her over to see her child. With her sister lived Fanny; a four-year-old girl and Kenneth aged nine, who was Louie's child from a previous relationship. According to the letter, Louie's sister promised to make all the necessary arrangements and pay all the expenses for the child which Louie claimed she was expecting. She said that she would stay with her sister, have the baby and then return.

On leaving she said, 'if I do not come back tonight, I shall stop and get it over. I think that will be about a fortnight.' Calvert left her home on the Monday morning and nothing was seen of her until 5 o'clock on 31 March when she returned with a baby. Her husband was delighted and rushed round to tell his sister who lived nearby. That first evening Louie Calvert said that she would not go to bed but would stay downstairs with her baby.

During her time away from the marital home, on 15 March, Calvert had her first encounter with Lily Waterhouse, asking if she knew of anywhere to stay as she had nowhere to go. She added that she was separated from her husband and had three children. Waterhouse said that she could stay with her.

Lily Waterhouse had lived in the same house for twelve or thirteen years on Amberley Road in a row of cottages between Tong Road and Oldfield Lane and was known in the neighbourhood for her eccentric habits; her husband passed away about a year before and she was lonely so was only too happy to give lodgings to Calvert. She did not have any children, though her mother was still alive and living in Norfolk.

A neighbour said that Mrs Waterhouse was a mystery.

She went out early in the morning but did not return until late at night or the early hours of the following morning. All sorts of people called at her home and often motor cars pulled up at the door. At one time she dabbled in spiritualisation and held what were called 'seances'.

When Calvert moved in she told a neighbour that her husband was a commercial traveller and that she and her family lived in Manchester. She added that she was in the area to suckle her baby and visit the infirmary and that she hoped that the family would soon move over to Meanwood.

On Tuesday, 30 March the Criminal Investigation Department had received a complaint from Lily Waterhouse. She said that various items were missing from her home and that she had found some pawn tickets in the house relating to some of her missing goods. She said that she suspected her lodger 'called Louise'.

On the evening of Wednesday, 31 March 1926, Lily Waterhouse was seen to enter her house, apparently in good health at about quarter-past-six. At about half-past-seven the same evening a noise was heard by her next door neighbour Mrs Clayton. She said it sounded as if someone was either erecting a bed or taking one down. An hour later at eight-thirty, Mrs Clayton saw Calvert leave the house with a child. When asked by Mrs Clayton about the noise, she replied:

Oh, we have been pulling down the little bed-chaff, getting ready for leaving on Saturday, and what we do not get out then, Mrs Waterhouse's brother will fetch out on Monday.

Mrs Clayton said that she thought she had heard Mrs Waterhouse making strange noises. 'Yes,' replied Louie, 'I have left her in bed crying because I am leaving her.'

Lily Waterhouse was due to attend the Magistrates Court the following morning concerning the theft allegations against Calvert but she did not turn up. Because of this, two officers turned up at her house later in the day, finding the house locked up. Nobody answered the door, so, having access to a key, the police entered the house and found the body of Lily Waterhouse

The Amberley Road house where Louie Calvert murdered Lily Waterhouse. The author

in a small upstairs bedroom.

Marks were found on her neck indicating that she had been strangled. Upon finding the body the officers noticed that a piece of string had been put over her feet and a mark was seen around her neck as if something had been tightly drawn across it. Similar marks were noticed on her wrists.

The police surgeon Dr Hoyland Smith immediately pronounced her dead and the police only had one suspect, especially as the murdered woman had already spoken to them about Louie Calvert. On the Thursday night detectives knocked on the Calverts' door at Railway Place, about a mile and a half from the murder scene. She was found to be wearing boots belonging to Waterhouse, which were several sizes too big for her. She was also carrying a suitcase full of items also belonging to the murdered woman.

Her husband, who had been so delighted about the new addition to the family was told that the baby which she had brought home and claimed as her own was actually born to a Pontefract woman and, as the arrest was made, Kenneth, who was staying with the couple, clung to his mother's skirt and screamed. The baby was taken away to the workhouse. The sequence of events staggered Calvert's husband who knew nothing of his wife's relationship with Lily Waterhouse, believing she had been in Dewsbury for the past fortnight.

Calvert admitted that she had been at Lily Waterhouse's home the previous night, but denied killing her and on the way to the station Calvert asked the officers: 'What is it about? Has she done herself in?' She later said: 'I wish I'd not called there last night.' When Detective Superintendent Pass charged Calvert at the station with the murder of Lily Waterhouse, she replied: 'It is a lie, I was in my own house at the time'.

After his wife's arrest, Arthur visited the Town Hall and had the news confirmed, that the baby was not Louie's, but the child of a seventeen-year-old girl. The letter, which Louie claimed was from her sister in Dewsbury was found to have a Leeds postmark and was written by Calvert herself. He came to realise that virtually all he had been told in recent weeks had been a pack of lies.

Louie Calvert came up for trial at Leeds Assizes with the case attracting great publicity. The prosecution, trying to make sense of Calvert's movements during the month of March 1926 alleged that having murdered Waterhouse she then took everything she could carry belonging to the dead woman. Among items found at Railway Place were two sheets with the name Waterhouse on them and found in her handbag was a key to the Amberley Road house, whilst she also had a scarf and chocolate box belonging to the dead woman.

The court heard that when police found the body of Mrs Waterhouse it appeared as if a struggle had taken place. Dr Hoyland Smith, the police surgeon examined the body of Mrs Waterhouse, first at the house in Amberley Road, then at Marsh Lane police station mortuary. At Amberley Road he found the body in a bedroom and noticed a deep pressure mark around the victim's neck. The mark, half an inch wide, must have been caused by something drawn around the neck.

There were also two large bruises on the head, one of which penetrated the skin and the hair was matted with blood. Some pieces of string and tape were found near the woman's feet and

Marsh Lane Police Station and mortuary where the body of Mrs Waterhouse was examined by the police surgeon. Leeds Library and Information Services

Dr Smith said that the cause of death was probably asphyxia by strangulation. He added that great force had been used.

The prosecution alleged and doctors' agreed that Mrs Waterhouse was first stunned and then strangled in the attack. A neighbour, Mrs Clayton said that on the night of 31 March she heard a noise in the little bedroom of Mrs Waterhouse's home. It was very faint at first but grew louder and was a kind of thumping sound like the heel of a boot or something that had fallen, which lasted for about quarter of an hour.

Sophia Morris of Railway Place saw Calvert at six-thirty on the morning of 1 April. Calvert was carrying a portmanteau, a bag and basket and Calvert told her she had been to the station to collect her luggage. In the basket were some cups and saucers which, Calvert said, her sister had given to her. She also said that her sister had given her some boots which were in her bag.

The jury did not deliberate for long in the case and Calvert was quickly found guilty and sentenced to death. In the wave of publicity which followed the case, a petition for the reprieve of Louie Calvert was set up and between 2,000 and 3,000 signatures were gathered including many from Ossett, Calvert's home town. However, it failed and the death sentence stood.

The day before Calvert died, she had a final visit from her husband and Kenneth. A number of people crowded round Arthur and his son with expressions of sympathy. Calvert's sister took Kenneth away from the crowd as he was still ignorant of the fact that his mother was about to die and that this would be the last time he would see her alive. Many of the women pressed forward and gave Arthur some money to give to his son.

Arthur Calvert, who despite the deceit of his wife, had stood by her, said of going to see Louie for the last time:

It was very hard on us, now that we knew there was no hope. It was hard on the little chap who didn't know what all the trouble was about. He had been told his mother was in London, and he thought he was in London seeing her.

Calvert had been resigned to her fate since the appeal had failed and she faced the prospect of a public hanging. Shortly afterwards she wrote to her sister-in-law. The letter said:

I only want to see my sonnie once again to kiss him goodbye then

I am satisfied. You have all done your best. God has not answered our prayers in the way we wanted. Still he knows which is best for me and I am quite prepared for the worst. Tell Kenneth to be a good boy and he shall see his mother again in heaven.

Calvert's sister-in-law, Hannah McDermott accompanied Arthur and Kenneth to the prison for the final visit. She said that Louie had accepted her fate and was bearing up remarkably well. When Calvert saw Kenneth she threw her arms around him and McDermott added:

For quite a while she held her boy on her knee, and chatted with him, and answered his little questions quite cheerily. When he asked 'when are you coming home mummy?' she just kissed him on the lips and said 'soon my boy'. When Calvert was asked, towards the end of the visit, to come clean and admit her crimes she once again protested her innocence, saying: 'I have not done it.'

Thomas Pierrepoint executed Louie Calvert on 26 June 1926 at Strangeways Prison, Manchester, the first woman to be executed at the prison since 1886. She was only the second woman sentenced at Leeds Assizes to suffer the death sentence, the other being Emily Swann who was the subject of a double execution at Armley on 29 December 1903 with James Gallagher. Calvert was also the first woman to be executed in England since January 1923.

The hour of the execution had been set for nine in the morning and well before that hour a number of people were at Strangeways to witness the execution. About 500 were there in total; most of them women.

At eight in the morning the two women warders who were looking after Calvert told her to stand up and she was taken by the arms and had her wrists strapped before being led out of the cell and to a point over the divide of the trap doors. She was supported whilst leather straps were applied to her ankles and thighs. Then Pierrepoint withdrew the safety pin and pushed the metal lever away from him. The trap doors opened and the body of Louie Calvert dangled in the cell below.

The body hung there, motionless, the head drooping from side to side as the medical officer went down to listen to the weakening heartbeat. Her death had been instantaneous and it

Strangeways Prison, Manchester. The author

was also confirmed by the autopsy that she was not pregnant. Her body was buried within the prison grounds. Many of the crowd were in tears when the bell tolled to indicate that Calvert had died.

Calvert was said to be upset that the case had not attracted great coverage from the press. She wanted to be in the limelight for the one and only time of her life, but was to be disappointed. Much of this was due to the General Strike which was headline

Strangeways Prison, Manchester. The author

THE STRANGE HISTORY OF LOUIE CALVERT.

WHAT THE POLICE FOUND.

FACTS THAT WERE REPORTED TO HOME OFFICE.

The possibility which "The Yorkshire Evening Post" has disclosed of a connection between Mrs. Calvert, the woman executed at Manchester yesterday, and the mysterious death of a Leeds man four years ago, may be supplemented by some further facts which we have gleaned to-day.

Investigations regarding the matter began with the Leeds police, at the request of the Home Office.

As we stated yesterday, Mrs. Calvert confessed to the crime for which she has been hanged. In her confession, taken down in writing and sent to the Home Secretary, she made mention of matters which were referred to the Leeds police for investigation. Her references were indefinite, but the Home Office considered that investigation should be made.

In particular, the police obtained particulars from the City Coroner regarding an inquest on the body of a man found drowned in the canal near Water Hall, Leeds, nearly four years ago. It was on July 12, 1922, that a policeman recovered from the canal the body of a man, subsequently identified as John William Frobisher, of Mercy Street, off Wellington Lane, Leeds. A peculiarity which was remarked on at the time, and which has since afforded an extraordinary coincidence, was that Frobisher had no boots. In that respect the case was similar to that of Mrs. Waterhouse, the victim of the crime for which Mrs. Calvert was hanged, and it will be recalled that when she was arrested, Mrs. Calvert was wearing a pair of boots which were identified as belonging to Mrs. Waterhouse.

Newspaper article on 'The Strange History of Louie Calvert.' Yorkshire Evening Post

news at the time and pushed the case onto other pages. There are no photographs of Calvert, mainly because her family were too poor to afford a camera and also because newspaper photographers were either on strike or failed to get an opportunity to photograph her during the trial.

The three-week-old baby which Calvert had adopted became a central figure in the story. She lay crying in her cot at Beckett Street poor law institution and news about the murder charge came as a great shock to the baby's mother and her parents. Ward said she regretted that her circumstances did not allow her to keep the baby and she hoped to hear from respectable people who wanted to adopt her.

Dorothy Ward eventually found a good home near Halifax. The publicity given to the little girl led to a number of people wanting to adopt her, leading to difficulty in choosing the suitable foster parents.

In the days following the execution of Louie Calvert the media of the time featured her in relation to the Frobisher case. Police who were involved in the death of Lily Waterhouse and that of John Frobisher were alerted to the fact that both had been found with their clothing intact apart from their boots. Whilst she was in prison, Calvert said that she had been worried for some time about the death of a man to whom she had acted as housekeeper before she was married. However, when questioned she refused to elaborate.

His death had been attributed to a drowning accident, but one of the officers who worked on the case remembered that Frobisher had been discovered minus his boots and it was that peculiarity which first linked Calvert with the Frobisher case; within days of her death police were convinced that she was responsible for the murder of John Frobisher.

Chapter 3

Double Execution at Armley 1864

In September 1864, the first, and final public execution took place at Armley Gaol. James Sargisson and Joseph Myers had both been found guilty of murder and despite both murders having been committed in other parts of Yorkshire, the cases attracted great publicity in Leeds, with the national media becoming involved in the story when it became clear that the two would be executed together. As a result unprecedented crowds flocked to the jail to see history in the making.

Joseph Myers, aged forty-five, was a saw-grinder from Sheffield. His wife Nancy was a year older and the couple had several children, though only two were living at home at the time the incident took place. It had been an unhappy marriage for some time; Myers was a heavy drinker with an evil temper whilst his wife was a hard-working woman who stayed with her husband, one suspects out of loyalty rather than true love. Myers often satisfied his craving for drink with money taken from his wife.

Events reached a head, or rather a foot, on 10 June 1864 and seems to have begun over an argument about a pair of Nancy's boots! On that morning at about nine o'clock, Nancy, fully dressed, went downstairs with the exception of one boot which her husband was holding. He ran downstairs and threw it at her. In a rare fit of temper she replied that if he did not like it, he could ram the boot down his throat. Nothing further was said and Myers went out.

When he returned he was seen in the yard, ushering his wife back into the house. He had threatened her many times previously, but this time words were accompanied with awful deeds and he attacked his wife, stabbing her several times in the chest with a scissors blade. She was seen by a neighbour staggering out of the house with blood pouring from her throat

Execution poster for James Sargisson and Joseph Myers. Leeds Library and Information Services

and face. A doctor rushed to the scene but she died about ten minutes later. Myers then tried to kill himself by cutting his throat but he survived, leaving a gaping wound and was taken to Sheffield Infirmary.

Though bleeding from the throat wound, Myers was conscious and asked a police officer, en route to the infirmary: 'Is she dead; I've done it and I hope she'll die.' Whilst in hospital, very weak and breathing heavily from a cough, he was charged with the wilful murder of his wife Nancy. The blade which caused the fatal wounds was later found in the house, having been thrown by Myers into a tub.

Myers pleaded not guilty when the case went to trial. He never denied that he killed his wife, though he claimed that he was under the influence of drink at the time. However, the jury found him guilty of murder and Myers was sentenced to death. Asked by the judge if he had anything to say, Myers replied:

I was drunk the night before. I had had a quart of ale the morning I committed the deed. My wife said she would have me committed to prison. I did not know what I was doing though I should not have killed her.

James Sargisson, aged twenty, did not have a police record until the attack on John Cooper on Saturday, 9 April 1864. Having spent time working in farming, he had appeared during the past year to have fallen, as the language of the day would have had it 'into idle and careless habits'. On the night of 9 April, John Cooper, aged twenty-seven, who worked as a gardener, was returning to his parent's home in Stone near Rotherham. On his way he called into *Mottram's Beerhouse* at Brookhouse to meet some friends. He had four glasses of ale and left at about ten o'clock in the evening. Sargisson was also in the pub along with some others and noticed the watch Cooper was wearing and the money he had in his possession.

When Cooper left the pub and continued to walk towards his parent's home, Sargisson and the other men attacked him with repeated blows from a hedge stake. After beating the man to death, he was robbed of his watch and money.

The following morning his body was found in grass by the roadside near to Roche Abbey. He was covered in blood and had sustained a fractured skull and a broken jaw. His eyes were black and his hands were covered in bruises, caused by trying to defend himself against the sustained attack. Lying next to him was a large hedge stake which had been pulled out of the hedge about fifty yards from where the body had been found. The grass near the body also indicated that a fierce struggle had taken place.

Cooper was powerfully built, standing over six feet tall and police believed he had been attacked by several men who had intended to rob him. When he resisted, they grabbed the hedgestake and killed him. His pockets had been emptied and been left inside out.

A reward was offered to anyone who could offer the police information on who had committed the crime, but almost a month elapsed before the police were ready to charge anyone for the murder. They apprehended Sargisson who admitted that he had been present when the attack took place, but denied murdering Cooper. He told officers where they would find the watch and other items stolen from Cooper on the night of the murder and named two other men, Denton and Taylor, who he said were responsible for the murder, adding that Denton struck the fatal blow.

He repeatedly declared his innocence, saying at the trial that he did not strike the final blow, though he admitted his involvement in the attack. However, the jury did not believe him and he was found guilty of murder. In Armley Gaol awaiting death, Sargisson protested his innocence, going so far as to deny any part in the attack. He said that he had not punched or kicked Cooper and accounted for blood found on his trousers by saying that they were stained whilst he was looking for his hat.

Both Myers and Sargisson were placed in Armley Gaol while they waited for appeals to be lodged on their behalf. However, these failed to reduce the sentences, so both men were forced to await their execution. Joseph Myers was still suffering from the severe wound to his throat which occurred when he tried to commit suicide immediately after killing his wife and there were real fears at the prison that the wound may re-open at any time and especially at the execution itself. He was given medical

Cartoon showing prisoners arriving at Armley Gaol. West Yorkshire Archive Service

attention in prison and the prison surgeon applied a plaster, which he hoped would last until the date of Myers' death. The *Leeds Mercury* reported that 'surgical skill' was used to save him for a 'just end'.

As the end neared for both men they became weaker with Sargisson having to be given stimulants in the days leading up to his death.

Askern, the executioner, came to Leeds from Doncaster on the Friday and stayed in the gaol throughout the night. At intervals during the evening and up until midnight, groups of

Prisoners at Armley Gaol. West Yorkshire Archive Service

policemen were marched up to Armley and a force of about two hundred remained on guard from midnight to the hour of execution. Among the crowds of people already assembled on the Friday and who came throughout the night, were those who had travelled on foot from the villages in the neighbourhood. Others made the journey from the Sheffield area, the region in which both crimes occurred.

Both Myers and Sargisson went to bed just after midnight, Sargisson not even bothering to undress, but both slept well, waking up around five o'clock in the morning. The two had breakfast two hours later and in the meantime they were engaged in a 'composed state of mind, in religious exercises'. Sargisson spent his last hour lying down, reading the bible, while Myers gave the governor Mr Keene, two sixpences, saying that he wanted Mr Godson, a Sheffield minister to give one each to his two youngest children.

The two men were oblivious to the frenzy which was enveloping the outside of Armley Gaol. There were already hundreds of people searching for a vantage point on the Friday evening and by Saturday morning, thousands were flocking to the area.

The *Leeds Mercury* reported:

> *The morbidly curious were to be met with in groups in every lane in the vicinity of the gaol, and every hedge and wall from which there was any prospect of obtaining a view of the spectacle was attempted by those who were choice in their selection of a position. The unseemly platform which had been erected in the field on the right hand and below the scaffold, and that which, with equally wretched taste had been placed on the roof of the toll-gate keeper's house in the road, were also occupied, notwithstanding the caution as to their insecurity made by the Mayor, who had not, unfortunately, the power to forbid their erection.*

As the hour of the execution approached, yet more people

Jailers at Armley working under the direction of a prison guard. West Yorkshire Archive Service

flooded into the immediate vicinity of the prison. The roofs of nearby houses and mills were popular vantage points as were the tops of lamp posts. In total, there were approximately 100,000 people present to watch the executions.

Apart from the open space in front of Armley Gaol, there were several hundred spectators on the Burley Road and near Woodhouse Moor, though that was a little too far to witness the execution first hand. The papers speculated on the type of people who came to witness this type of 'occasion'. It said that in the main they were men employed in mills, factories and workshops with 'a not inconsiderable sprinkling drawn from a lower and more degraded Stratum of Society, but embracing a few of what were called 'the respectable class.'

With a crowd of approaching 100,000 it was rather optimistic to expect respectful silence and there were moments throughout the Saturday morning when laughter rang out from the crowds. The papers were disapproving of the frivolity commenting,

> ...the more thoughtless of the mass indulged in jests, and others even so far forgot the solemnity of the event as to engage in games of 'thimblerig' and 'fly the garter'.

However, the atmosphere was generally quiet and orderly and many listened to the Scripture readers who, mounted upon stools, read the lessons.

Preparations at the prison for the execution were completed on Saturday morning. The scaffold had been erected during Friday, but it was not until Saturday morning that the black cloth screened its limbs, which to some extent was also to hide the men when they stood upon the drop, from the crowd beneath.

The bell of the gaol rang out at five minutes to nine on the Saturday morning, which led to a huge cry of 'hats off!' from the crowd present. The crowd then saw the Under Sheriff along with Mr Keene. Following behind was the chaplain repeating the funeral service. The two prisoners followed, both looking pale and supported either side by warders. Sargisson and Myers knelt upon the drop whilst Reverend Henry Tuckwell, the chaplain continued to read the service. Both men uttered responses when prompted and regularly interrupted the service

Cartoon showing a prisoner in a cell at Armley Gaol. West Yorkshire Archive Service

DOUBLE EXECUTION AT LEEDS.

THE execution of Myers and Sargisson—the one for wife murder at Sheffield, and the other for killing John Cooper, at Laughton, near Roche Abbey—took place at Armley gaol, on Saturday morning, in the presence of a crowd variously computed at from 80,000 to 100,000. Before retiring to rest on Friday night, and also on Saturday morning, Sargisson again earnestly declared that he did not strike the fatal blow, but that he participated in the plunder; and his statement obtains the full credence of the prison officials. He threw himself on the bed without undressing; and when he was visited at six o'clock on Saturday morning, the Governor found him stretched on his couch, and engaged in reading his Bible. Myers rose about the same hour, having slept soundly; and he handed to Mr. Keene, the governor, a piece of paper, in which were two sixpences, and which he wished Mr. Godson, a minister from Sheffield, to hand to his (Myers) two children. Fears were entertained that the wound in the throat of Myers (inflicted after he murdered his wife) might open, and as far as possible to prevent such an occurrence, Mr. Price, surgeon to the gaol, applied plaster to the wound. About this time, both the prisoners appeared very exhausted, and before the pinioning Sargisson was so weak that stimulants had to be administered. Myers was exceedingly pale, but appeared to be more resigned to his fate. During the process of pinioning, Sargisson turned to Myers and said, "Are you happy?" and the latter replied "Yes, I am." At five minutes to nine the bell of the gaol began to toll. There was immediately, from the dense multitude in front, a cry of "Hats off," and almost immediately the Under Sheriff and Mr. Keene passed from the door to the scaffold, followed by the Chaplain repeating the funeral service. Immediately behind him, supported on each side by warders, were the two prisoners, pale and anxious-looking. They knelt upon the drop, whilst Mr. Tuckwell, the chaplain, continued to read the service. Both of them uttered the responses and frequently ejaculated "Lord have mercy upon me," and "Lord save my soul." The executioner then stepped forward and adjusted the rope upon Myers, and after that upon Sargisson. Myers appeared quiet, but Sargisson shook his head and breathed heavily. Both of the men continued to call out "Lord save me," and the last words uttered by Sargisson were to his brother murderer. He called out, "Art thou happy, lad?" to which Myers responded, "Indeed I am." Instantly, with a solemn thud, the drop fell, and the bodies were immediately completely hidden from the crowd. Myers seemed to die almost immediately, but the other man struggled violently for about two minutes. Sargisson, to the last, adhered to the statement which he had made throughout. Askern, of York Castle, was the executioner.

Report on the double execution. Bradford Observer

with cries of 'Lord, have mercy upon me' and 'Lord save my soul'. As the pair were being put into position, Sargisson turned to Myers and asked 'Are you happy?' 'Yes I am' came the reply.

After the service was completed, Askern of York Castle stepped forward and placed a white cap over the heads of both men and adjusted their ropes. Myers was calm but Sargisson appeared tense and was seen to be breathing heavily. Both continued to call out 'Lord save me' before both uttered their final words, Sargisson once more asking Myers 'Art thou happy lad?' Myers replied 'Indeed I am'.

Myers had intended to talk to the crowd but was persuaded not to, largely because the severe wound to his throat would have meant that much of what he would have said would not have been heard by the large crowd. As an alternative he prepared a statement which he gave to Mr Godson to publish:

I am heartily sorry that I have committed such a dreadful deed – done in the heat of passion and excited by drink, so that I did not know what I was doing until I came to the Infirmary and had been there some time. I hope that God Almighty will forgive me for Jesus Christ's sake. One of my dear children expressed feelings to me when they visited me in Leeds prison, that it would be a nice thing for us to have it thrown in our faces that our mother was murdered and our father was hanged, but I hope and trust there is not such a hard hearted being upon the face of the earth to tell these poor orphan children of their parent's faults. Signed Joseph Myers.

Once the words were uttered the drop fell with a thud and the two bodies were hidden from the crowd. Myers appeared to die immediately whilst, Sargisson struggled for about two minutes.

The crowds soon dispersed, though some remained until ten o'clock when the bodies were cut down. A few minutes before, the upper portion of the screen had been removed so as to allow those spectators who had remained behind, to see that the execution had indeed taken place.

Upon examination of the bodies it became clear that the fears regarding Myers' throat had been justified. The result of the sudden drop led to the wound being torn open, leaving the throat with a hole large enough to place a pocket-handkerchief into. Blood continued to pour from the wound for some minutes after the drop fall. In accordance with the sentence, the bodies were buried within the precincts of the gaol.

In amongst the huge publicity generated by the double execution and the incredible crowd who gathered to witness it, there were dissenting voices. Canon Edward Jackson, from St James's and a friend of the Reverend Henry Tuckwell who was with Myers and Sargisson prior to their deaths was one who voiced his disapproval. He wrote in the *Leeds Mercury* on 19 September 1864:

On Saturday week there was the awful execution, our first in Leeds which, whilst it caused a deep sensation over all the town, affected me and my people all the more, in that the good chaplain has for long been a voluntary curate at St James' one whom we deeply respect; so that his trouble and anxieties were ours.

Alas! What a sad and I may say horrible, picture of humanity was then exhibited. I allude not to the wretched culprits so much, as to the fact of the vast crowd gathered together to gaze on their dying agonies, and the utterly revolting deportment showed by the larger portion of those comprising it.

The chaplain, the Rev. Henry Tuckwell, who has suffered so much in preparing these men for their doom, is himself fully convinced, both as regards the condemned criminals and the whole body of prisoners in the gaol, that the sentence of imprisonment for life would have been viewed with comparative indifference, whilst the execution brought a thrill throughout the whole place, and in the case of the sufferers was preceded by the marks of what we believe to have been the truest penitence.

Chapter 4

Peace in Our Time
1879

Leeds was the last resting place of double-murderer Charlie Peace who told a clergyman who had an interview with him in prison shortly before his execution that he hoped that, after he was gone, he would be entirely forgotten by everybody and his name never mentioned again. Little chance of that, as Peace stands out as one of the great personalities among English criminals of the nineteenth century.

On 4 February 1879, Charlie Peace appeared at the Leeds Assizes, accused of the murder of Arthur Dyson. Whilst at Armley he also confessed to the murder of PC Cock in Manchester, which another man was serving time in prison for. Such was the interest in the trial that admission into the public gallery was by ticket only. Over two hundred people crowded into the courtroom, leaving over a thousand disappointed people outside.

The life of Peace was dominated by crime and he frustrated the police for over twenty years until his execution. His crimes took in Sheffield, Manchester and London, and though he did not commit crimes in Leeds, the city is his last resting-place and it is well worth recalling his reign of terror.

Charlie Peace was born in Sheffield on 14 May 1832, the son of a shoemaker. He acquired a limp when he was injured while apprenticing at the Millsands Rolling Mill. A piece of red-hot steel pierced his leg, leaving him with a permanent limp and he was forced to spend about eighteen months in Sheffield Infirmary. The injury (he also suffered a wound to his hand) left him with little enthusiasm for work and he embarked on a life of crime, even though, as a young man he was quite musical and enjoyed playing the violin, becoming known as 'The Modern Paganini.'

His first crime was the stealing of an old gentleman's gold watch, but he soon graduated onto larger crimes and his first brush with the law occurred on 26 October 1851 when he broke into a Sheffield house, stealing a large number of items. Some of the goods were later found on Peace when he was arrested; though, owing to a good character reference given on his behalf by his employer, he was let off lightly with a month's imprisonment.

Peace took to wandering from town to town, though in 1859 he found time to marry Hannah Ward, a widow with a son. Whilst keeping a 'front' of employment as a joiner, Peace spent much of his time as a cat-burglar and a thief. In June 1859 he was arrested for a burglary in Rusholme, Manchester, and was sentenced to six years in jail.

On his release he changed his name to George Park and called himself a 'professor of music', however, he was still intent on a life of crime and on 21 August 1866 he was arrested for two burglaries in Victoria Park, also in Manchester. He told police that he was called George Parker and that he was a carpenter. In court he was sentenced to seven years in prison.

Whilst serving this sentence Peace made a dramatic bid for freedom whilst in Wakefield prison. When working on some repairs in the jail he managed to smuggle a small ladder into his cell. With the help of a saw made out of some tin, he cut a hole through the ceiling of the cell, and was about to get out on to the roof when a warder came in. The warder tried to grab the ladder but Peace knocked him down, ran along the wall of the prison, fell off on the inside owing to the looseness of the bricks and slipped into the governor's house where he changed his clothes, and waited there for an hour and a half trying to find the chance of making an escape. However, he failed and was recaptured in the governor's bedroom.

When Peace was eventually released from Wakefield, he initially tried to make a life for himself away from crime and spent the next two or three years making an honest living by setting up shop as a gilder and picture-framer in Britannia Road, Darnall. Peace and his wife, Hannah were settled in Sheffield, but Peace was not one for a life of domesticity and he

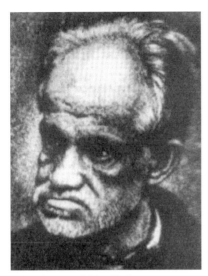 

Two pictures of Charlie Peace. Author's collection

soon began to become aware of an attractive woman by the name of Katherine Dyson.

Katherine lived with her husband Arthur as neighbours of Peace in Britannia Road and he became known to the couple, first as a tradesman and then as a friend. Charlie was a small man, five feet, four inches tall, wiry, agile and strong and he appeared to have a permanent scowl etched onto his face. He was not, by any stretch of the imagination, good-looking as existing photographs confirm. Arthur Dyson was tall and well-mannered, the complete opposite of Peace in many ways, and it is not known what Katherine, tall, young and buxom, saw in Charlie, but they visited music-halls and pubs together and had a short affair.

The relationship, such that it was, did not last long and by June 1876 Arthur Dyson had become annoyed with Peace coming to his house, asking for Katherine and told him, in no uncertain terms, to stay away from his family. Peace responded by leering in through their windows and by threatening Katherine with a gun. In retaliation Dyson threw a card into the garden of Peace's house on which was written: 'Charles Peace is requested not to interfere with my family.' Peace continued to threaten the couple and in a desperate attempt to try and end the dispute the Dysons' obtained a magistrate's warrant for Peace's arrest. This had the desired effect and Peace and his family fled to Hull where he briefly opened an eating shop.

He did not stay in East Yorkshire for long and before the summer of 1876 was out, Charlie Peace set up home back in Manchester. Addicted to crime, Peace set off for Whalley Range, a fashionable suburb of Manchester on 2 August 1876 with the intention of breaking into a house.

On his way he came across two policemen and before he was able to get into the grounds of a house, Peace was confronted by one of the officers. He jumped onto a wall but when he fell onto the other side, he landed in the arms of the second officer who was waiting there for him. Peace shouted: 'You stand back, or I'll shoot you'. The officer refused so Peace fired a shot in order to frighten him. The officer charged at him with a truncheon and the two men fell to the ground in a scuffle. Peace fired his gun again, this time shooting the officer in the chest. PC Cock fell to the ground and died from his injuries.

Two Irish brothers named Habron were arrested and tried for the murder at Manchester Assizes, though John Habron was acquitted on Monday, 27 November. The case against William Habron depended to a great extent on the fact that he, as well as his brother, had been heard to threaten to 'do for' PC Cox and shoot the 'little bobby'. In July 1876 the murdered policeman had ordered summonses against the two brothers for being drunk and disorderly and the two men had sought retribution.

Other evidence against Habron included the fact that the other constable on duty with Cock stated that a man he had seen lurking near the house about twelve o'clock on the night of the murder appeared to be William Habron's age, height and complexion, and resembled him in general appearance. Also, the boot on Habron's left foot, which was 'wet and sludgy' at the time of his arrest, corresponded in certain respects with the footprints of the murderer. Alas, Habron also had no alibi and the jury convicted him of the murder whilst recommending mercy. The Judge without comment sentenced him to death, though thankfully, this was changed on appeal to penal

The Banner Cross *public house*. The author

servitude for life. Charlie Peace had the audacity to attend the trial at Manchester Assizes, and watched impassively from the public gallery as the judge passed the sentence.

The morning after the trial, on 29 November 1876, Peace left Manchester and returned to Sheffield where his mother still lived. He surprised her by walking in to her house, saying that he had come to Sheffield for a fair. By the afternoon Peace was in an Ecclesall pub, entertaining the customers by playing tunes on a poker suspended from a piece of strong string, from which he made music by beating it with a short stick. The musician was rewarded by drinks and it did not take many to get Charlie Peace drunk!

Arthur and Katherine Dyson had moved to Banner Cross Terrace in the city, off Eccleshall Road and Peace was in that area by evening with the intention of rekindling his relationship with Katherine. He made his way to the Dyson's house and, looking in through the window, saw her putting her son to bed. Shortly afterwards, while sitting outside the house, he cracked his fingers and gave a low whistle to attract her attention. Katherine took a lantern and went to visit the closet where she was confronted by Peace who called on her to persuade her husband to withdraw the warrant against him. Katherine became angry and began shouting at Peace. In a fit of rage he

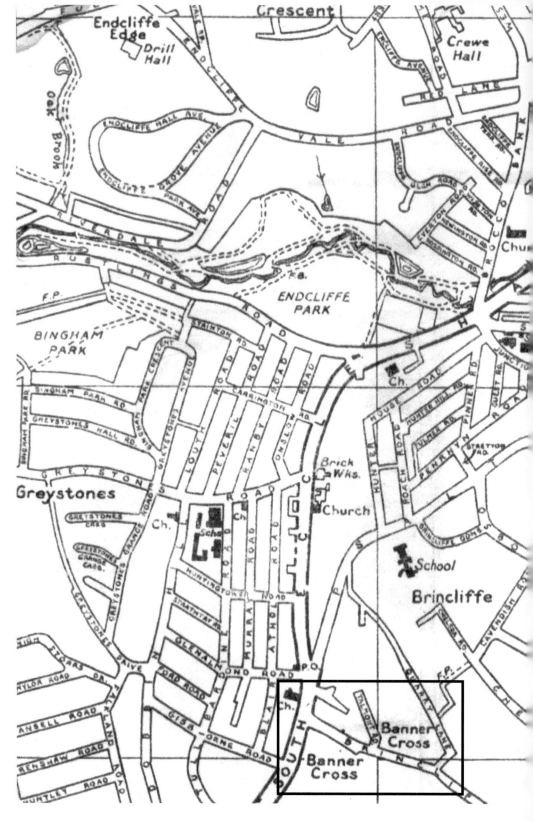

Map of Sheffield showing the Banner Cross area. The author

drew his revolver and said:

Now, you be careful what you are saying to me. You know me of old, and know what I can do. I am not a man to be talked to in that way.

Katherine shut herself away in a tiny outbuilding and began to shout. Hearing the noise, Arthur Dyson came rushing out of the house and chased Peace down a passage and into a nearby street. He got hold of Peace who shouted at Dyson to let him go. When he refused, Peace got out his gun and fired a warning shot. The two men wrestled each other to the ground and Peace managed to get to his feet and shoot directly at Dyson.

Katherine had come into the yard upon hearing the first shot and rushed to her husband's side calling out: 'Murder! You villain! You have shot my husband.' Dyson had been shot in the temple and despite medical attention, he died two hours later.

Peace panicked. He wanted to try and persuade Katherine Dyson to stay with him but people had started to gather on the street, alerted by the noise of the fight and the shots having been fired. He decided there was no other option but to, once again, run from the scene of a murder.

First port of call was Hull where Peace's wife was still running the eating shop. He stayed in the city for three weeks, changing both his name and his appearance. He shaved off his beard, stained his face with walnut juice and wore glasses. By now police were linking him with the Dyson murder and there was a price of £100 on his head. A description of him was circulated by the police:

Charles Peace wanted for murder on the night of the 29th inst. He is thin and slightly built, from fifty-five to sixty years of age. Five feet four inches or five feet high; grey (nearly white) hair, beard and whiskers. He lacks use of three fingers of left hand, walks with his legs rather wide apart, speaks somewhat peculiarly as though his tongue were too large for his mouth, and is a great boaster. He is a picture-frame maker. He occasionally cleans and repairs clocks and watches and sometimes, deals in oleographs, engravings and pictures. He has been in penal servitude for burglary in

Manchester. He has lived in Manchester, Salford, and Liverpool and Hull.

Peace left Hull and burgled his way down the country eventually settling in Evelina Road, Peckham with his new girlfriend, Susan Grey. The couple passed themselves off as Mr and Mrs Thompson and he resurrected his musical playing, developing a fine reputation for musical evenings, where he played the banjo or the violin.

Peace was also a keen inventor and at the time of his final capture he was working on a smoke helmet for firemen, an improved brush for washing railway carriages, and a form of hydraulic tank. Socially 'Mr Thompson' became quite a figure in the neighbourhood. He was a regular attender at the Sunday evening services at the parish church and was well regarded in the neighbourhood.

Hannah Ward and her son had left Hull and were installed in the basement of the 'Thompson's' house. It was an unusual arrangement and, not unexpectedly, the two women were soon constantly bickering. It was enough to drive a man from his house and though Peace had a good reputation in the local area, due to his musical prowess, he soon returned to his old habits and the house became richly furnished through his 'ill-gotten gains'.

However, the life Peace had begun to enjoy was about to come to an end. Following the spate of burglaries in the Blackheath area, several of them committed by Charlie Peace, the police were out in force on the night of Thursday, 10 October 1878. PC Edward Robinson noticed a light in the rear rooms of 2 St John's Park and summoned assistance. When a sergeant and another constable arrived the three men went to investigate. The sergeant went to the front door and rang the bell while the two constables watched the rear of the house.

Peace jumped out of the drawing-room window and was pursued across the garden by PC Robinson. Peace turned and warned Robinson to stay away or he would shoot. He fired three shots at the policeman, missing the man's head. Robinson charged at Peace and he fired a fourth shot which also missed. With a cry of 'You bugger, I'll settle you this time'. Peace fired again and the shot entered the policeman's arm just above the right elbow. By this time the other officers had arrived and they overpowered Peace, who was hurt in the process. Property stolen from the house and housebreaking equipment were found on Peace.

Peace gave his name as 'John Ward' and he appeared at the Old Bailey, under that name on 19 November 1878 on a charge of attempted murder. It took the jury just four minutes to find him guilty and he was sentenced to penal servitude for life. Police brought pressure to bear on 'Mrs Thompson' and she revealed to them who 'John Ward' really was. Peace was charged with Dyson's murder and once it was established that the man in question was Charlie Peace, he was committed for trial.

A manacled Charlie Peace was taken on Friday, 17 January, from Pentonville to Sheffield to face the murder charge at the magistrate's hearing. The hearing was adjourned and he was taken back to London but on the following Wednesday he returned to Sheffield by train for the resumption of the hearing.

From the start of the journey he had made himself a nuisance to the guards who accompanied him, making excuses for leaving the carriage whenever the train stopped. The two warders provided him with little bags which he could use when he wished and then throw out of the window. Just after the train passed Worksop, Peace asked for one of the bags and when the window was lowered to allow the bag to be thrown away, Peace, with lightning agility, took a flying leap through it.

One of the warders caught him by the left foot, but Peace, hanging from the carriage, grasped the footboard with his hands and kept kicking the warder as hard as he could with his right foot. The other warder, unable to get to the window to help his colleague, was making vain efforts to stop the train by pulling the communication cord.

For two miles the train ran on, Peace struggling desperately to escape and at last he succeeded in kicking off his left shoe, and he fell onto the line. The train ran on another mile until, with the assistance of some passengers, the warders were able to get it stopped. They immediately hurried back along the line, and there, near a place called Kineton Park, they found Peace lying on the ground, barely conscious and bleeding from a severe wound in the scalp. A slow train from Sheffield stopped to pick up the injured man and as he was lifted into the guard's van, he asked them to cover him up as he was cold.

On arriving at Sheffield, Peace was taken to the Police Station and made as comfortable as possible in one of the cells. Even then he had enough about him to be difficult over taking the brandy ordered for him by the surgeon, until one of the officers told him they would have none of his hanky-panky, and he would have to drink it.

Peace's trial for the murder of Arthur Dyson opened on 4 February 1879 at Leeds Assizes before Mr Justice Lopes. Mr Frank Lockwood, defending Peace, tried to prove an 'extra-marital relationship' between Charlie and Mrs Dyson but she denied this throughout.

Throughout the trial Peace maintained that he did not intend to kill Dyson and thought that he was still alive when he left the scene. He said that he thought of trying to help him up, but people were starting to gather so he made his escape. He added that in both murders the struggle to get away was the cause of him missing his aim and committing murder. Of the Dyson case, he said:

I do not deny that I took Mr Dyson's life, as it turns out, but I did not go there with the intention of doing it. It was as unintentional a thing as ever was done; and it would not have been done if I had not been interrupted in trying to get Mrs Dyson to induce her husband to withdraw the warrant, and if Mr Dyson had not been so determined to get me into trouble and prevent my getting away.

The trial lasted nine and a half hours, but when the jury retired it took them just twelve minutes to find Peace guilty and he was sentenced to death. In prison, Peace said: 'If it had not been for Mrs Dyson taking out that warrant against me and causing me to leave home, there would have been no Manchester and no Banner Cross murder.'

The day before his execution, his wife Hannah Ward, her son Willie and some friends of the family visited Charlie Peace. He was weak and resigned to his fate by this time. The Central

New Wortley Cemetery with Armley Gaol in the background. The author

News Agency reported:

> *The convict Peace continues very restless in his cell, and since the departure of his relatives in the afternoon had taken no food. The chaplain is still with the condemned man, affording him such consolation as is possible. Under the circumstances an extra number of warders have been told off for duty outside the walls by night, and the Chief Constable has been requested to furnish a large force of police for duty outside the prison this morning.*

Though he was prepared for death, Peace retained some of his great spirit; disagreeable to the last, on the morning of his execution he even complained of his last breakfast saying: 'This is bloody rotten bacon!'

At his execution Peace wore the same convict dress as he had when he appeared at Sheffield and on trial in Leeds. He did not see the gallows until the procession took a sharp left turn, but when he did, his face, which was pale and haggard, changed colour. As his legs were being strapped and a noose was placed around his neck, he was about to have a cap put around his face until Peace turned to the executioner and said: 'Don't, I want to look.'

As the moment of his execution grew ever-nearer Peace called out to members of the press who were present:

You reporters, I wish you to notice the few words I am going to say to you. I know that my life has been base and bad, but I wish you to notice, for the sake of others, how a man can die, as I am about to die, in the fear of the Lord. Gentlemen, my heart says that I feel assured that my sins are forgiven me; that I am going into the kingdom of Heaven, or else to the place prepared for those who rest until the great judgement day. I do not think I have any enemies, but if there are any who would be so, I wish them well. Gentlemen, all and all, I wish them to come to the kingdom of Heaven, when they die, as I am going to die.

After addressing the officials with his last goodbyes, Peace turned back to the reporters and uttered his final words:

My last wishes and my last respects are to my dear children and their dear mother. I hope none will disgrace them by taunting or jeering them upon my account, but to have mercy upon them. God bless you, my dear children. Goodbye. Heaven bless you all. Goodbye. Oh my Lord God, have mercy upon me.

On 26 February 1879, the *Leeds Mercury* reported:

Peace's career has ended. At eight o'clock yesterday morning he died upon the scaffold. The ground was white, and snow fell lightly at intervals, but as the hour of the execution neared a gradually increasing throng assembled around Armley Gaol. Beyond the arrival of the deputy sheriff and the representatives of the press, and the hoisting of the black flag indicating the law had secured its victim, there was nothing to be seen, but several thousand of the lower classes braved the biting weather to gratify a morbid curiosity.

A reporter inside the gaol added:

> *...upon a slight signal Marwood pulled upon a lever by which the treacherous platform opened downwards, and the body dropped quickly out of sight with a dull heavy thud. In a moment or two all was over and life was extinct.*

When the time came, his death was swift. The body remained suspended at the gallows for about an hour before being cut down and removed to another part of the prison. Shortly after the inquest, Peace was buried within the precincts of the prison.

After Peace had been found guilty of the Whalley Range murder, a movement was set in place to release William Habron from prison. Peace himself spoke of the trial and conviction of Habron after he was sentenced to death. He said:

> *This greatly interested me. I always had a liking to be present at trials, as the public no doubt know by this time. People will say that I was a hardened wretch for allowing an innocent man to suffer for the crime of which I was guilty but what man would have given himself up under such circumstances, knowing as I did that I should certainly be hanged? Now that I am going to forfeit my own life and feel that I have nothing to gain by further secrecy, I think it is right in the sight of God and man to clear this innocent young man.*

Article showing the execution of Charlie Peace. Bradford Observer

Habron was subsequently set free after the Home Secretary granted permission. He was given a pardon and £800 compensation.

The Times newspaper reported that, since Franz Muller murdered Briggs on the North London Railway and the poisonings of William Palmer, no criminal case had created such excitement in the public mind as that of Charles Peace. A large tableau of Peace and Marwood, his executioner, soon appeared in Madame Tussuad's waxworks, depicting the execution scene.

Chapter 5

Horsforth Tragedy –
The Murder of Barbara Waterhouse
1891

O f all the murders we hear about, the murder of a child is one likeliest to stir the emotions and one only has to recall the Moors Murders, Jamie Bulger and the Soham murders to judge the impact such horrific crimes have on the public at large. It was no different in the nineteenth century.

Barbara Whitham Waterhouse lived in Horsforth with her parents. She was five-years-old and a happy little girl. Barbara was playing outdoors with a friend on Saturday, 6 June 1891 and was seen playing in a yard at about one o'clock in the afternoon, peering into a shop window in Town Street, Horsforth. The last words she was heard to utter were as she was gazing at some advertisements in a grocers shop window. She remarked of a man in costume: 'That looks like my dada.'

Ethel Whitham, who was playing with Barbara, was asked by

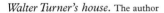

Walter Turner's house. The author

The Black Bull *public house, Horsforth. Barbara Waterhouse spent part of her childhood here.* The author

her mother to go and fetch some ham sandwiches and the two girls collected them before going their separate ways and between Saturday afternoon and Wednesday, 10 June nothing was seen nor heard of Barbara.

Her parents reported her missing and sightings of Barbara started to come into the police, including one at Horsforth Station on the Saturday afternoon in the company of another girl. About an hour later she was reported to have been in the same area and, also on the Saturday afternoon, a girl fitting her description was seen in Woodside heading towards Leeds in the company of a man and a woman.

However, hopes faded and the worst fears of Barbara's parents, family and friends were confirmed when news came through that a body had been found. The body of five-year old Barbara Whitham Waterhouse was found behind the Municipal Buildings in Leeds on Wednesday, 10 June 1891. The *Yorkshire Post*, published the day after the discovery of the body reported:

Nothing more foul and ghastly is remembered by the Leeds police to have occurred within the borough for thirty or forty years.

The paper commented on how the little girl's parents coped with identifying her body, saying: 'The mother fainted at the sight of her dead child and the father was all but unable to bear up amid his tragic surroundings.'

The murder took place at the time of the 'Jack the Ripper' murders in the East End of London and the Yorkshire newspapers made much of the similarities due to the mutilation of Barbara's body. There were forty-five different wounds on the body including cuts and stab wounds. The coroner, Edward Ward believed that the cause of death came from a deep gash which ran from the bottom of the stomach to the chest. It appeared to Ward that the murderer stabbed the little girl in the chest before ripping the body right up to the neck. Other injuries, which would have been fatal, occurred after the girl had died. Her throat was cut from ear to ear and her legs were cut and had almost been hacked away from the body. Cuts on the little girls fingers produced evidence that she had tried, in vain, to resist the sustained attack.

Then, as now, the murder of children was rare and the case shocked the people of Leeds and the surrounding area. Many people made their way to Alexander Street to the spot where the body was found; shocked that the location was so central, near to both the Town Hall and the police headquarters. The shock and horror was felt most keenly in Horsforth, the suburb of Leeds which was home to the dead girl's family. Up until the discovery of her body, people in the community clung to the belief that she had become lost and was being cared for until contact with her parents could be made.

The *Yorkshire Post* noted:

That the district had been exceptionally free from serious crime or outrage of any kind for years past only tended to increase the indignant horror experienced by the inhabitants. The shocking occurrence formed the sole topic of conversations during the day and at night parents seemed to have taken extraordinary precautions to keep their children within doors.

At the post-mortem, Barbara's father David, a quarryman, said

Alexander Street where the body of Barbara Waterhouse was found. The author

THE FEELING THROUGHOUT THE COUNTRY.

IS HE "JACK THE RIPPER?"

The interest which was manifested throughout Leeds and the district yesterday when the details of the horrible murder of Barbara Waterhouse were made known continues to increase and spread on every hand. Now inquiries are continually being made from all parts of England as to whether trace of the murderer has yet been found. Very hand abhorrence has been expressed at the horrible injuries which the diabolical murderer has inflicted on his poor innocent little victim, and in some districts the opinion gains considerable force

THE MURDERED CHILD.

Newspaper article showing a picture of the murdered girl. Leeds Mercury

that he had last seen his daughter at six o'clock on the Saturday morning, adding that she was a healthy, intelligent child who had never strayed too far from home. He confirmed that the shawl, in which the body was found, did not belong to anyone in his household.

Police Constable William Moss told the inquiry that he had found the body on the Wednesday night. He had passed the area around Alexander Street at 10.15 pm and had seen nothing, but when he returned to the area at 11.40 pm he found the bundle. On turning the bundle over and lifting the corner of the shawl he

Newspaper article on the murder. Leeds Mercury

saw a child's leg. The child was wearing a frock and petticoat with boots and stockings. The body was taken first to the Town Hall, then to Millsgarth Street Mortuary and PC Moss added that, with the help of witnesses, it had been established that the body must have been placed at the spot no earlier than 11.10 pm.

The police force wasted no time in trying to find the culprit though they were hampered by having few clues in the early stages and no obvious motive. Superintendent Stansfield and Detective Tidswell, both experienced officers, took charge of the operation to find Barbara Waterhouse's killer. They strongly believed that the murder did not take place in Horsforth, but somewhere between the village and the centre of Leeds, though others in the force thought that the killing took place in the centre of Leeds, at or near to the place where the body was eventually found.

Initial reports included the sighting of a man wearing a tall hat and carrying a suspicious-looking bundle on the Wednesday night. The police were also urged to investigate all caravan dwellers in the area with many feeling that Barbara was murdered by a tramp. Sightings of a girl with a man and a woman also aroused suspicion as the body had been washed after the murder and it was felt likely that it would have been the work of two people. Another piece of evidence supporting the possible role of a woman in the murder was the fact that the body was wrapped in a shawl when it was found. This led police to investigate the sighting of a woman in Horsforth on the Saturday afternoon selling 'fly-papers' though it was not known if she was wearing a shawl.

There was also a theory that the murderer may have intended to carry out the mutilation of the body even further in order to conceal the evidence, but lost the heart to do so, and resorted, instead, to dumping the body.

There were many theories flying around from many quarters, particularly as the case attracted so much interest from the people of Leeds, however, few fingers were pointed towards the residents of Horsforth. It was almost as if it had never occurred to the people of the village that the murderer himself was in their midst. As days passed there was real fear that the case would remain a mystery. However, help was soon at hand.

Walter Turner, aged thirty-one, a weaver by trade, lived in Horsforth with his mother, Harriet. She had been away from Horsforth for a few days but returned on the evening of Saturday, 6 June, the day that Barbara Waterhouse disappeared, bringing her grandson, called George Holder Joy.

Throughout the Sunday, Joy noticed that Walter Turner lay on the sofa which was placed in front of the coal-place in the kitchen of the house. It was in a different position from normal which made it impossible to get in or out of the coal-place. Also, a supply of coal had been placed near the fire, so that there was no need for anyone to go to the coal-place.

Harriet Turner became suspicious that the coal-place had suddenly become 'out of bounds' but Turner insisted that nothing was wrong. However, early on the Monday morning, before Turner woke up, she decided to have a look for herself. She peered into the coal-place with a lighted match and immediately her eyes fell upon the mutilated body of Barbara Waterhouse. She let out a terrible scream and ran upstairs to get some clothes on before leaving the house.

Turner heard the scream, leapt out of bed and stopped her from leaving. He told her that he had nothing to do with the body and that he would tell her about it afterwards. Reluctantly she decided to stay and later that morning, she went to the house of a neighbour called Mrs Gaulter who worked at the same mill as Walter Turner. She said that Walter would not be in work that day as he was not feeling well. Soon after returning home the two of them left the house carrying with them three bundles.

The following day a boy helped Turner to carry a box from his house at the Green in Horsforth to another in Back Lane. Turner said that the box contained his 'Sunday best clothes' and on the Wednesday evening, shortly before the body was found, Turner and his mother carried the same box to Newlay Station. They then took it by train to Leeds and then to a workshop owned by Thomas Joy in the White Swan Yard, off Crown Street.

Though Harriet Turner was helping her son in his bid to escape capture, her guilt was increasing and, in a state of desperation told a friend, Mrs Cotterill, of the discovery in the coal-cellar, saying: 'There's nothing less than murder in our house.' Mrs Cotterill and her husband, barely able to comprehend what they were hearing told Harriet to go down to the Town Hall as soon as possible and tell her side of the story.

However, probably out of loyalty to her son, she didn't go down to the Town Hall but instead joined her son in reclaiming the box from Joy's workshop. By this time it was late and the two of them went up Duncan Street, Briggate, Commercial Street and Park Row and then walked up Alexander Street. Walter Turner took the body of the missing girl out of the box and left it in the doorway of an entrance to the Municipal Buildings. The pair then went to Joy's house, taking the empty box with them before returning to their home in Horsforth.

By the time they had walked home, the body had been found by PC Moss, who took it to the Town Hall where it was examined by Police Surgeon Ward. It was soon established that the body was that of the missing girl and a mounted messenger was sent off to Horsforth to notify the parents. Ironically, the

Photograph showing the body and coffin of Barbara Waterhouse. The author

messenger passed Walter Turner and his mother as they were walking back to the village, however, they were not seen as they shrank into the shadow of a high wall.

On Friday, 12 June, two days after the discovery of the body, Harriet Turner took the empty box, which had contained the body of Barbara Waterhouse to the New Station in Leeds and left it on one of the platforms. She returned home only to find that her son was out. Taking this as her cue to confess all to the police she returned to Leeds and made a statement to the police. She found out that the reason Walter Turner was not home was because he had been arrested. The Cotterill's, realising that Harriet had not yet told the police, decided that they had to take action, leading to Turner being charged with wilful murder. Harriet was taken into custody on a charge of being an accessory to murder.

Walter Lewis Turner was in the dock at the West Riding Assizes, Leeds Town Hall on Saturday, 1 August 1891. Richard Rathmell, a witness, told the court that on the night on 7 June, he passed by the house occupied by Turner and his mother and heard sounds coming from inside the house as though someone was dragging a box about. Another witness, Thomas Myers, said that the following day he had seen Turner carrying a large bundle.

Edward Ward, the police surgeon said that when he visited the house in Horsforth, he did not find any bloodstains, but believed that the girl would have died within a few seconds of the wounds being inflicted on her body and said that though it was possible that the girl had been killed at the house of Turner, he thought it unlikely. He explained that blood would have certainly been in evidence on the floor or the walls and it would have been difficult for the murderer to leave no trace of the attack.

Mr Mellor, on behalf of Turner, argued that the evidence given by the prosecution lacked a vital chain that linked the accused to the murder. He said it had been proved that the Turner family did not know the family of the murdered girl and when Barbara had last been seen walking near Turner's house, she had been walking away from it. He also argued that there was not a shred of evidence that Turner had been out of the house after ten o'clock on the morning of 6 June. He added that nobody had ever seen Barbara enter the house of Turner and that during the six or seven hours in which it was assumed that the murder had taken place, there was nothing to link the accused with the subsequent attack.

Justice Grantham began summing up and said that the case against Turner depended upon presumption. He asked how the bundle containing the body of Barbara Waterhouse came to be in his house and concluded that if he did not commit the murder, he must have known who did.

The jury wasted little time in finding Walter Turner guilty of murder. Asked if he had anything to say to the court, the condemned man said:

I wish to assert my innocence as I have always done. I am not guilty and I shall always say so. Some of the witnesses could have testified that I have always been fond of children.

Justice Grantham then sentenced Turner to death followed by loud applause in the courtroom. Harriet Turner, tried by Justice Grantham before her son, was found guilty of being an accessory and was sentenced to penal servitude for life. She was then called as a witness against her son and her testimony, though given unwillingly, undoubtedly helped in Turner being found guilty of murder. Her sentence, which led to loud protests throughout the country, was subsequently reduced to twelve months' hard labour.

Right until the end Turner hoped for a reprieve, but it was not to be and no petition was waged on his behalf. The hoped for confession never came and he maintained, to the end, that he did not know how the body of the girl came to be found in his house.

Following a last night spent writing letters; Turner was hanged at Armley Gaol on Tuesday, 18 August 1891 without having confessed to the murder. The execution was carried out in private with no press admitted. The papers reported that, to the last, Turner retained the stolid, unmoved demeanour, which had been his conduct from the moment the death sentence was passed.

His last walk was taken firmly and the rope was quickly

The grave of Barbara Waterhouse in Horsforth Cemetery. The author

adjusted around his neck. Just before 8.00 am, the lever was pulled; the trap doors released and Turner died instantly. The black flag was hoisted on the central tower of the prison, which was received by cheers from the many people who had congregated near the prison gates. The body was allowed to hang for an hour, until about 9.00 am when it was taken down and examined by the doctor.

The prison's statement read:

W.L. Turner was hanged this morning, at eight a.m. in the new scaffold-shed adjoining the cookhouse. His death was instantaneous. A drop of from 8ft was given. He exhibited the same indifferent manner up to the last: he made no confession: ate well: slept well. The new hanging apparatus was used, and worked satisfactorily. Besides the gaol officials, three borough justices were present. Billington was the executioner.

Without a confession of any sort only two people knew how Barbara Waterhouse came to her death. Barbara herself and Walter Turner. With his death went the chance to find out exactly what happened.

What is clear is that somehow Turner saw Waterhouse, who had been separated from her friend on the streets of Horsforth and enticed her back to his empty house.

Turner in his statements to the police made no reference to what he was doing that afternoon; he tried to make people believe he was in bed fast asleep, however, other members of the family thought it would have been very out of character for him to go to bed, especially leaving the front door unlocked.

The police believed, and they had evidence on their side, that Turner enticed the girl into his house, killed her and, after draining the body of blood, placed it in the coal-cellar until it could be disposed of. His plans were interrupted when his mother found the body and from that point, he had to include her in his plans.

After he murdered the girl, the blood was probably drained down the sink, though curiously no blood was found when the drains were searched. Once the body had been drained of blood, it was wrapped in the shawl and put in the coal cellar. On the Saturday night Walter Turner slept in the same room as

George Holder Joy and when Joy awoke he found that his uncle had lit a fire; an unusually large one as it was June and the weather was warm. Clearly, Turner's motive for lighting such a large fire was to dispose of any evidence that remained in the house.

An intriguing twist to the tale was that Mrs Turner was a superstitious woman who often dreamt of cats before a tragic event took place. On the Sunday night she did indeed dream about cats and came downstairs as she couldn't sleep. It was then that she found the body and it is quite possible that if she had not have had the dream, she would not have gone downstairs and the following day Turner would have found a way of disposing of the body. As it was, Turner's deadly secret was uncovered and the murderer was brought to justice.

Chapter 6

Murder at Star Fold
1900

The address of 7, Star Fold in Beeston was home to Charles and Mary Ann Blewitt, a couple who had been married for four years. Most people who knew them assumed it to be a happy marriage and few who saw Mary Ann as she washed her step on the morning of 8 June, thought it would be the last time they saw her alive.

A neighbour, Mrs Harrison saw Mary at about nine o'clock that evening. However, about a quarter of an hour later, the same neighbour noticed the Blewitt house with the blinds now drawn and the house shut up.

The blinds were not opened again before 17 June. Though a number of people went to the house in the meantime, nobody was unduly concerned; assuming the couple had gone away for a few days. Jemima Bunney, Charles Blewitt's mother visited the house on several occasions only to find it shut. On one occasion she persuaded a man to take a ladder up to a top window, but it was fastened and he was unable to get in.

On 17 June, Jemima was beginning to get anxious as she had some possessions in the house, which she wanted to collect, and she persuaded her husband and the landlord, Thomas Armitage to go with her. Armitage decided to break down the door and climbed into the house. In a chair in the front room was the body of Mary Blewitt. Her throat had been cut and her clothing was covered in blood. On the table were the remains of an unfinished meal.

Police were on the scene within minutes and established that Mary Ann Blewitt was almost certainly killed where she was found and that in addition to her throat having been cut, she also had cuts to her wrist and hand. Suicide was discounted and it became clear that she had been taken off her guard, as there were no signs of a struggle having taken place.

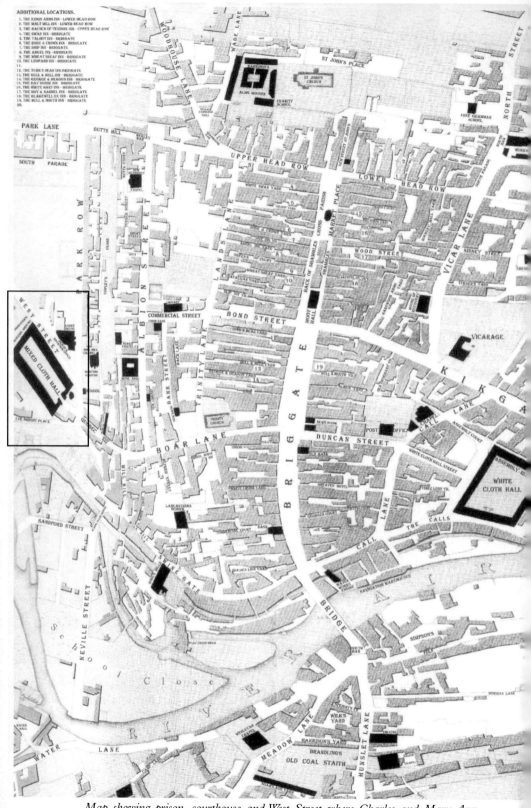

Map showing prison, courthouse and West Street where Charles and Mary Ann Blewitt lived. N. & F. Giles plan of the town of Leeds, 1815

Police sergeant Wilkes undertook a search of the house and found a shoemaker's knife with small stains on the handle in a cupboard. There was also a newly sharpened razor in a drawer and a bloodstained purse was found under the fireplace. Three carving knives and two hatchets, all recently sharpened, were also found in the house.

On 1 July a second search of the house by the police revealed a revolver and a marriage certificate showing that the couple had been married on 20 August 1896. A note beside it read: 'Please save these marriage lines for me while I want them. Your sister, Mary Ann Blewitt, No 7, Star Fold, Beeston.' Her brother, George Jackson said that Mary Ann had given the gun and marriage certificate to him, but had asked for them back recently, leading to concern about the state of her marriage.

The last person to leave the house on 8 June had been Charles Blewitt and the thirty-three-year-old tanner had not been seen in Beeston since. Though close to his mother, he did not tell her he was going away, nor did he take any spare clothes with him.

The hunt for Blewitt began in earnest and local gossip went into overdrive. The local theory was that he had drowned

Leeds in the eighteenth century, The Thoresby Society

himself, but police stuck to their task and believed that he was working under an assumed name in a pit in the Barnsley area.

Blewitt had been seen on the day he disappeared going into a hairdressers in Beeston where he had his moustache and a week's growth of beard removed. He was also spotted on Halifax Road at 3.30 am on 9 June. Constable Blackburn noticed a man walking towards Halifax and asked him what he was doing so early in the morning. The man said he had come from Morley and was going to Heckmondwike to try and find work.

Blewitt was eventually traced to Halifax when some men told police that their new workmate fitted the description of the wanted man. On 3 July Blewitt turned up for work at the Redman Brothers foundry and was arrested in the manager's office. He gave his name to the police as Oliver Jackson but when asked what his name was before he came to Halifax, he hesitated and said, 'well, my name is Charles Blewitt.' He was immediately arrested and charged with the wilful murder of his wife. He was remanded in custody, the legal process eventually taking him before the dock at Leeds Town Hall on 30 July.

The Crown Court at Leeds Town Hall was packed to capacity at the West Riding Assizes on Monday, 30 July 1900 for the trial of Blewitt. The prosecution in the case suggested that, although the evidence against Blewitt was circumstantial, it was overwhelming. Mr Heald, the police surgeon confirmed to the court that the jury was looking at a murder case rather than suicide. He added that various knives and other sharp instruments in the house were found stained with blood and added that Mary Ann was murdered with the assailant standing behind her.

The jury failed to come to a unanimous verdict on the Thursday night and was discharged, so Blewitt was re-tried the following day before a new jury.

There was a good deal of interest in the re-trial with the public galleries crowded and the new jury heard Mr Banks open for the prosecution. He said that as this was a murder investigation, Charles Blewitt had to be the main suspect. There had been no break-in at the home, so it had to be someone so trusted that he was able to get behind Mary Blewitt and get the blade to her throat before there was any struggle.

Banks added that on the same night as Mary Ann was killed, Charles Blewitt fled from the house, changed his appearance and used another name, that of Oliver Jackson. The only possession he took from the house was a razor.

William Sydney, a neighbour of the Blewitts' told the court that about a fortnight prior to 8 June, he had heard Mary tell her husband to go out and look for work. There was then a noise which sounded, to Sydney, as if someone had fallen downstairs. He then saw Mary Blewitt run out of the house.

Dr Heald, the police surgeon told the court that Mary Blewitt would have died very soon after the wound to her throat had been inflicted, so suicide was impossible as she would have had no time to have thrown the weapon away. The doctor also said it would have been impossible for the woman to have caused the injuries to her wrist and hand after the cut to her throat. The wounds were consistent with the woman having put up her hands in an effort to protect herself from attack. He added that the shawl must have been placed over the body once the blood had nearly stopped, and, therefore, once the woman was dead.

James Edward Smith had worked for the toolmakers in Halifax at the same time as Blewitt. He said that he had seen the report of the murder in a paper and asked Blewitt if he came from Leeds. Blewitt said that he did but when asked if he knew about the Beeston murder, had replied, 'I do not come from that quarter.' He said that he had not seen the reports in the paper as he was not a good scholar and did not read much. When asked about the case by another workmate, Blewitt said that he had not been in Leeds at the time of the murder and had never been married.

Mr Waugh, for the defence expressed his amazement that a man, who had never been in trouble with the police in the past should suddenly become a murderer. He explained the shaving off of the moustache by saying that Blewitt was in Halifax looking for work, so it was natural that he should try to smarten himself up. He added that Blewitt left Beeston without giving rise to suspicion; when in Halifax he freely admitted that he came from Leeds and pleaded with the jury that it was better that a hundred guilty men should escape rather than one innocent man be wrongly convicted.

Jemima and James Bunney, Charles Blewitt's mother and stepfather told the court that it was not unusual for Blewitt to shave off his moustache and that Mary and Charles were a happy couple.

The Judge, in summing up, asked the jury to dismiss the idea of suicide and to just consider the matter of whether or not Charles Blewitt was the murderer. After forty-five minutes the jury returned a verdict of guilty. Asked if he wanted to say anything to the court Blewitt declined.

Addressing Blewitt the judge said:

Charles Oliver Blewitt, the jury after a careful trial and after hearing the most able defence by your counsel, have found you guilty of the crime with which you are charged. I have only to say I agree with that verdict. You will have an opportunity, which you denied your victim, of making preparation for your great change. It only remains for me to pass sentence of death.

The Home Secretary later confirmed the sentence, thus ending any hopes Blewitt had of the death sentence being reduced to life imprisonment. He had been hoping for a reprieve but showed little emotion when being told the news. Though on good terms with the warders, he never spoke about his wife or the horrific events of 8 June. On 18 August he wrote a last letter to his mother and father. It read:

My dear mother and father, I received your letter this morning, and was pleased to hear from you, but was sorry to hear that grandfather was so ill. When you come you might all come at one time. You can come when you can make it convenient for you to do so, and I hope that Ernest and Lizzie will do so. Give my regards to all the family, from your loving son, Charles O Blewitt.

Though a religious man, during his final days in prison he avoided the prison chapel as he did not want to be stared at by the other prisoners. He had a meeting with the minister of the prison during his final hours and was asked, once again,

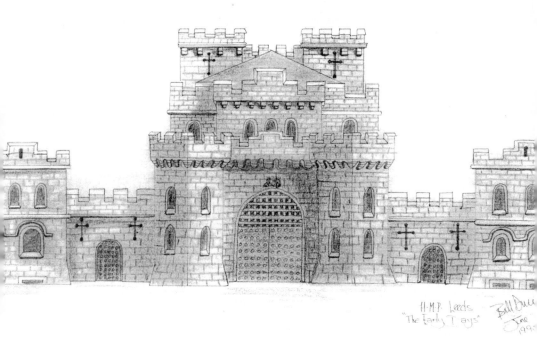

HMP Leeds 'The Early Days'. West Yorkshire Archive Service

Cartoon showing prisoners at Armley Gaol. West Yorkshire Archive Service

about the death of his wife. However, he refused to answer any questions about the murder and added, 'Well, I suppose I should have to die sometime or other, so it doesn't bother me.'

Blewitt made his own way to the execution chamber on the morning of his death and did not make a statement to the gathered press. Before the prison clock had finished chiming the hour of nine o'clock, the black flag was hoisted, telling the large crowd who had gathered, that the execution had been carried out.

A few hours later, the inquest into the death of Blewitt was carried out within the prison, which stated that death was instantaneous. Due to his refusal to discuss the events of 8 June, any hope that the public would find out his motive for the killing died at the execution chamber along with Blewitt.

Chapter 7

A Watery Grave
1900

The murder of two young sisters in Leeds was a shock
to the local community, more so as the murderer was
their father. A local newspaper called the case 'a sordid
tragedy' and its ramifications were felt by many.

Six-year-old Ada and four-year-old Annie were the daughters
of Thomas Mellor, aged twenty-nine, who was a labourer from
Holbeck. Their mother used to live with them but subsequently
'lost her mind' and was moved to Menston Asylum where she
died in 1899. Ada herself was in poor health. She had a disability
and had often been for treatment at the Leeds Infirmary.

After their mother's death the children, and Mellor, went to
lodge with a neighbour called Pricilla Redshaw and though the
woman did her best to look after the children; keep them clean
and fed, Mellor took little interest in their welfare. He earned
about seventeen shillings a week from his job, but instead of all
the money going to provide for his family, much of it was spent
on his passion for horse racing. Pricilla found it difficult to make
ends meet and she went out cleaning in a bid to raise money,
though it was not enough to keep herself and the children in
food, or pay the two shillings a week rent.

Their home was in a terrible state and broken windows were
stuffed with rags. Priscilla had even sent her own two children to
live with her mother so that she could spend more time with
Mellor and his daughters. However, the rent began to fall
further into arrears and the situation became so bad that the
family were forced to leave the house, pulling together their few
belongings. No other house was available to them so the family
had to use a disused stable to store bedding and their meagre
possessions, which consisted of a few sticks of furniture.

By day, Redshaw and the two children would pass their time
in the squalid court where they used to live, talking to

neighbours while Mellor was at work. At night the bedding was taken from the stable to the old house where they were able to rest until the morning.

On the Friday, the morning before the bodies were found, Mellor gave Pricilla Redshaw eight shillings to spend on the family and the resentment Pricilla felt grew even stronger. She urged him to hand over more of his money to provide more food and shelter for the family rather than wasting his wages on gambling and drink. Mellor stormed out the house but Redshaw felt that the situation had become intolerable and she took Ada and Annie to a nearby pub where Mellor was drinking. She left the children with him, saying she was leaving. He responded by saying that he would go to the bottom of the water with them, but Redshaw took little notice of the remark at the time.

Mellor spoke to Esther Ann Mellor, his sister-in-law after Pricilla left him and she asked him what the 'poor little children' were going to do, as a result of the family being made homeless. Mellor replied that the water was big enough to hold both of them. He added: 'I have said it, and it will be tonight.' At just before eleven on the Friday night he was seen with the children in Fourth Court and had said to another neighbour, Mary Bramham that he did not know what to do with the children.

Mellor saw the Holbeck Guardians as the last chance to find some shelter for his daughters. By now desperate, he explained the situation to them, but they refused, believing that Mellor had enough money to secure accommodation for him and his family.

The bodies of Ada and Annie were found in the Leeds and Liverpool Canal at Holbeck at about five o'clock on the Saturday morning, on 12 May 1900, by a man called William Wilson. He was walking by the canal in Globe Road when he noticed two objects floating in the water. Taking a closer look, Wilson was horrified to find that they were the bodies of two small children.

Wilson called the police and the bodies were taken, first to Hunslet Road police station, and then to the Millgarth Street mortuary to await identification. It appeared that the bodies had not been in the water very long and the police were quickly of the belief that they were sisters owing to both of them having red

The canal at Globe Road where the bodies of Ada and Annie were found. The author

Millgarth Street police station and mortuary. The bodies of Ada and Annie were taken here for identification. Leeds Library and Information Servicees

Water Lane and Bridge Road, where Mellor was arrested and taken into custody. The author

Hunslet Road police station. The bodies of Ada and Annie were first taken here. Also, Thomas Mellor was charged with their murder here. Leeds Library and Information Services

hair and some facial similarities.

Police investigations took them to Fourth Court passage and yard in Bridge Road, Holbeck. The passage was situated near to the London and North West railway bridge and consisted of a few cottages, many of them in a ramshackle state. Mellor, who also had red hair, was arrested at the corner of Water Lane and Bridge Road and was taken into custody.

At Hunslet Road police station, he was charged on suspicion of wilful murder and was later brought up before the city police court on the charge. He claimed that he had been unable to afford accommodation for his family though, when arrested, Mellor was found to have sufficient money on him.

The police court heard from a witness, James Alfred Metcalf, who said that at five to eleven on the Friday night he had seen a man on the canal bank with two children in his arms. Mellor was also spotted about half an hour later in Wellington Street seeking lodgings and without the children. Thomas Walker, a restaurant keeper in Wellington Street confirmed the sighting, saying that Mellor had gone to his house at eleven-thirty at night on May 11 asking for lodgings. He managed to get a bed and left the house at eight o'clock the following morning.

Police constable Ernest Rodgers, who was on duty in the cells at the Town Hall on Sunday had special charge of Mellor. He told the court that at five-thirty on the Sunday afternoon he had heard the prisoner begin to cry and Mellor told him that he wanted to give a statement to the police. He said that he had taken the children to the workhouse and offered to pay for them, but the authorities would not have them. He had then taken the children into the lane to try and find a bed for the night but could not find anyone to take them in and then admitted that out of desperation he took them to the canal and pushed them in.

Rodgers asked, 'and threw them in?' Mellor replied, 'No, shoved them in.' Rodgers replied, 'It is a wonder they didn't scream.' Mellor said, 'The first one was very quiet but the other was the strongest and youngest and cried out 'Oh dada!'

Mellor was remanded in custody and sent for trial at the West Yorkshire Assizes at the end of July. For the defence, Mr Marshall contended that a case for a verdict of murder had not been made, adding that Mellor had placed the girls in the water in the expectation that they would scream, attract attention and promptly be rescued before they were drowned. He argued that this made a verdict of manslaughter more realistic.

Mellor told of his desperation when it was his turn to address the court. He said:

> All I have to say is I tried my very utmost to get them a home from about seven o'clock in the evening up to eleven. I went before the Holbeck Guardians a fortnight since this afternoon to see if they would take them in the Workhouse, and I would pay for them. The chairman, however, said they could not do anything for me.

The court heard that the Holbeck Guardians did not consider Mellor as in a state of destitution and, therefore, refused his request. He then asked his brother to take in the children, but, as he was also without a place to live, he had no success.

In the summing up the judge said that Mellor was deserving of at least some sympathy. He had failed to find lodgings on that night and had also applied to the Guardians for accommodation for the girls. However, he argued that whatever the circumstances, Mellor did push the girls into the canal. He said there were other alternatives open for Mellor such as leaving them in the street where they would eventually have been found.

The jury retired to consider the verdict and after a gap of seventeen minutes returned to court to find Mellor guilty of murder with a unanimous recommendation of mercy. They added that in their opinion, if the Guardians had taken the children in, as Mellor had asked, the affair would not have occurred. Curiously, Mellor was found guilty of the murder of Ada, but not guilty of the murder of Annie, despite there being little doubt that he pushed both girls into the canal. The judge rejected the jury's plea for mercy and Mellor was sentenced to death.

Asked if he had anything to say, Mellor said he thought that it was a very unjust sentence:

> I do not see how the jury can convict on the evidence of one lying constable. I have no more recollection of making the statement than the paper on the wall. If I have made it I ought to have some recollection of it. I don't think there is one spectator in court who will agree with this verdict.

Postcard view of Armley Gaol. Leeds Library and Information Services

The judge assumed the black cap and said:

> *You have been convicted, and I think properly, of the murder of practically your two children, although the form of the accusation is of one only. The jury has accompanied their verdict with a recommendation of mercy, to mercy upon grounds which are worthy of consideration. It will receive consideration of the proper quarter, to which I shall forward it.*

Mellor was led out of court in a dazed manner. He took the news badly and was distraught in his last few days in the condemned cell at Armley Gaol. His father and stepmother visited him in these last few days and found him in poor health, largely as he was not eating properly. He continued to tell his visitors that he never thought it would come to this.

Mellor hoped for a reprieve right up until the end. A large signed petition had been arranged on his behalf after the jury's recommendation for mercy at the trial. It contained several thousand names but, tragically for Mellor, it was forwarded too late and the Home Secretary's decision was communicated at exactly the same time as the petition was being despatched to him.

Mellor was executed on 16 August 1900 on a grey day in Armley. The weather did not prevent the usual crowd of people turning up to witness the hoisting of the black flag and at exactly nine o'clock in the morning the flag of death was risen up the flagstaff where it remained for an hour. The execution took place in private, meaning that representatives of the press were excluded. Though invited to make a statement prior to his death, Mellor stayed silent, as did Charles Backhouse who was executed at the same time.

The case of Charles Backhouse involved the murder of a police officer. Police constable Kew attended an incident at Swinton, Yorkshire, on 10 July 1900. The incident was close to where Charles Backhouse lived and, when Backhouse saw the officer, he drew a pistol and shot PC Kew dead. It transpired that twenty-three-year-old Backhouse bore a grudge against the constable after he had arrested Frederick Backhouse, his eighteen-year-old brother, for assaulting Charles' wife. Both of the brothers were arrested and charged with murder, but only Charles was found guilty.

Chapter 8

The Yorkshire Witch
1807

Mary Harker was born at Aisenby, near York, in 1768. Her father was a farmer and both parents were well respected in their local community but Mary began stealing from an early age and seemed uncontrollable. She left the family home for the first time in 1780 when she went to Thirsk, finding work as a servant before arriving in York in 1787. However, less than a year later she was found stealing some property belonging to her mistress and was forced to flee once again, this time to Leeds.

She left her clothes and wages behind in York and for some time she stayed in Leeds without any friends or a job. Eventually, on the recommendation of a friend of her mother, she was given a job in the shop of a mantua maker. Mary was quite successful and supplemented her income by becoming a soothsayer.

At the age of twenty-four, Mary met a wheelwright named John Bateman and after only three weeks courtship, the couple were married in 1792. They managed to find furnished lodgings in High Court Lane, though Mary's criminal past did not end with her marriage as she robbed a fellow lodger and obtained goods by deception. The thieving continued and the couple were soon constantly on the move to escape accusations of theft.

In 1796 a fire at a local factory led to many deaths and Mary went to a charitable lady, Miss Maude, pleading for linen sheets to lay out her child, who had, she claimed, perished in the inferno. The sheets were given and Mary took them to the local pawnbroker's. The success of this venture seems to have fired her imagination and she posed as a nurse at the General Infirmary and collected old linen for dressing wounds. She took these to a pawnshop and realised that there was money to be had through deception.

With her husband in the supplementary militia by this time, Mary was left to her own resources and in 1799 she moved to Marsh Lane, near Timble Bridge in Leeds where she began fortune-telling and selling charms.

She claimed to customers, that one of her hens was remarkable as it laid an egg with the inscription 'Crist is coming'. She then forced up two other eggs into the ovary of the poor hen, which bore similar inscriptions and were deposited in the nest.

Mary's activities continued apace. In September 1803, she went to help two maiden ladies, called Kitchin, who owned a linen draper's shop. One of the ladies fell ill and Mary went to fetch medicine from the doctor's. The lady died within the week and within the next ten days, the other sister and their mother had also died. However, Mary's part in their demise was never proven. Mary claimed that they had all died from the plague, or possibly cholera, but she padlocked the door as soon as the last hearse had left and when the creditors came to sort out the estate, both the house and the shop been plundered.

By 1807, after numerous moves, the Bateman's eventually settled in a house on Meadow Lane, but Mary's deceit continued. A lady called Judith Cryer was concerned about the behaviour of her eleven-year old grandson. Mary said that she would write to a fortune teller, in Scarborough, called Miss Blythe and a letter soon appeared with a gallows and rope on it, which said that the boy would hang before his fifteenth birthday unless the woman could raise four guineas.

Instructions came from the fictional 'Miss Blythe' saying that Cryer should sow three of the guineas into a leather bag. This was to be placed in her bed and was not to be opened until the boy was fourteen. Mary did this for her and to pay for the cost of postage, Judith Cryer agreed to clean for Mary for three months. However, when Mary was later arrested, Judith Cryer opened the bag and found it contained nothing.

It was Mary's involvement with the Perigos' in 1806 that led to her eventual downfall. Rebecca Perigo, of Bramley, had fallen ill with pains in her side and was told by a doctor that it was caused by an 'evil wish'. Rebecca and her husband William were

High Court Lane. Mary Bateman lived here in the early 1800s. The author

Meadow Lane as it stands today. Mary Bateman lived here in the early 1800s.
The author

recommended to Mary and they told her that a neighbour had cast a spell on Rebecca.

Bateman began corresponding with the couple though most of the letters were written in her guise as Miss Blythe. She told the couple that Miss Blythe was a friend from Scarborough who could 'read the stars'.

In October 1806 the couple received this letter purporting to come from Miss Blythe of Scarborough:

> *My dear Friend – You must go down to Mary Bateman's at Leeds, on Tuesday next, and carry two guinea notes with you and give her them, and she will give you the other two that I have sent to her from Scarborough, and you must buy me a small cheese about six or eight pound weight, and it must be of your buying, for it is for a particular use, and it is to be carried down to Mary Bateman's, and she will send it to me by the coach -- This letter is to be burned when you have done reading it.*

From this time until March 1807, a great number of letters were received by the Perigos' demanding that they send a number of items, as well as money, to Miss Blythe through the medium of Mary Bateman. In the course of the same period, money to the amount of almost £70 was paid over. Mary Bateman also requested a live goose in order that it might be used as a burnt offering.

In March 1807, the following letter arrived:

My dear Friends – I will be obliged to you if you will let me have half-a-dozen of your china, three silver spoons, half-a-pound of tea, two pounds of loaf sugar, and a tea canister to put the tea in, or else it will not do -- I durst not drink out of my own china. You must burn this with a candle.

Another letter followed a month later:

My dear Friends – I am sorry to tell you you will take an illness in the month of May next, one or both of you, but I think both, but the works of God must have its course. You will escape the chambers of the grave; though you seem to be dead, yet you will live. Your wife must take half-a-pound of honey down from Bramley to Mary Bateman's at Leeds, and it must remain there till you go down yourself, and she will put in such like stuff as I have sent from Scarbro' to her, and she will put it in when you come down, and see her yourself, or it will not do. You must eat pudding for six days, and you must put in such like stuff as I have sent to Mary Bateman from Scarbro', and she will give your wife it, but you must not begin to eat of this pudding while I let you know. If ever you find yourself sickly at any time, you must take each of you a teaspoonful of this honey; I will remit twenty pounds to you on the 20th day of May, and it will pay a little of what you owe. You must bring this down to Mary Bateman's, and burn it at her house, when you come down next time.

Another letter arrived at the Perigo's house on May 5:

My dear Friends – You must begin to eat pudding on the 11th of May, and you must put one of the powders in every day as they are marked, for six days – and you must see it put in yourself every day or else it will not do. If you find yourself sickly at any time you must not have no doctor, for it will not do, and you must not let the boy that used to eat with you eat of that pudding for six days; and you must make only just as much as you can eat yourselves, if there is any left it will not do. You must keep the door fast as much as possible or you will be overcome by some enemy. Now think on and take my directions or else it will kill us all. About the 25th of May I will come to Leeds and send for your wife to Mary Bateman's; your wife will take me by the hand and say,

'God bless you that I ever found you out.' It has pleased God to send me into the world that I might destroy the works of darkness; I call them the works of darkness because they are dark to you – now mind what I say whatever you do, This letter must be burned in straw on the hearth by your wife.

Miss Blythe also ordered different amounts of money to be paid to Mary Bateman who would then put it into small bags and leave the bags around the house. She said that if either William or Rebecca opened any of the bags the charm would be broken and they would suffer instant death. However, after eighteen months had expired they would be able to open the bags and claim back the money.

Rebecca duly baked a pudding using some of the powder given to her by Mary Bateman. It tasted awful and William could only manage one mouthful; his wife ate three or four mouthfuls before being violently sick. Despite this they still ate the puddings on the days stated by 'Miss Blythe', in fear of the consequences if they did not do as ordered.

Both of them fell sick, especially Rebecca who was taken violently ill. She took the honey, as directed by 'Miss Blythe' but did not recover and she refused to have a doctor come to the house in case the charm should be broken. William slowly recovered his health but Rebecca persisted in taking the honey and lost strength daily. Her tongue became swollen and her mouth became an unusual black colour. She died on 24 May, her last words being a request to her husband not to be 'rash' with Bateman.

Thomas Chorley, the Leeds surgeon saw Rebecca just after she died and immediately came to the conclusion that poisoning was the cause of death; his belief strengthened when a cat died soon after eating some of the pudding. However, no further steps were taken and William Perigo even continued corresponding with Bateman. When hearing of the death of Rebecca Perigo, Bateman told William that his wife's death was due to her having eaten all the honey at once.

At the beginning of June, Perigo received another letter from Miss Blythe. It read:

My dear friend – I am sorry to tell you that your wife should touch of those things which I ordered her not, and for that reason it has caused her death; it had likened to have killed me at Scarborough, and Mary Bateman at Leeds, and you and all, and for this reason, she will rise from the grave, she will stroke your face with her right hand, and you will lose the use of one side, but I will pray for you. I would not have you to go to no doctor, for it will not do. I would have you to eat and drink what you like, and you will be better. Now, my dear friend, take my directions, do and it will be better for you. Pray God bless you. Amen. Amen. You must burn this letter immediately after it is read.

Bateman, through the guise of Miss Blythe continued to write letters to Perigo demanding clothing, coals, and other items. By October 1808, two years having elapsed since the commencement of the charm, Perigo became increasingly suspicious of Bateman. He searched the little silk bags in which his notes and money had been [as he believed] sewn up; but although the bags were in precisely the same positions in which they had been placed by Rebecca, there was nothing in the bags but rotten cabbage-leaves and bad farthings. Confronting Bateman with this information she said: 'Aye, this comes of being in too great a hurry; you have opened them [the bags] too soon.' 'Too soon, did you say?' shouted Perigo, 'I think I have opened them too late.'

The darkness finally fell from William Perigo's eyes and he arranged to meet Bateman at the side of the Leeds/Liverpool canal in order to give her more goods. William Duffield, Chief Constable accompanied Perigo and duly arrested Mary Bateman for fraud. She was questioned by Magistrates and committed to York Castle on the suspicion of the wilful murder of Rebecca Perigo.

Her house was searched and almost all the property sent to the supposed

Mary Bateman.
The author

Miss Blythe was found in her possession. A bottle containing a liquid mixed with two powders; one of which proved to be oatmeal, and the other arsenic, was taken from her pocket when she was taken into custody.

The case went to trial on 17 March 1809. The examination of the witnesses, who were called to support the case for the prosecution, showed that Mary Bateman lived in Leeds, and was well known in the city and surrounding districts, as a 'witch'. She had been in demand to work cures of 'evil wishes', and other customary imaginary illnesses and was known throughout the Leeds area as 'The Yorkshire Witch'.

The evidence against Bateman showed that there was no such person as Miss Blythe and that all the letters she claimed had been sent by her were in Bateman's own handwriting and had been sent by her to Scarborough to be transmitted back again. It was also proved that she tried to buy arsenic at a shop in Kirkgate in April 1807.

Thomas Chorley, the Leeds surgeon, gave evidence at the trial. He said that he had analysed what remained of the pudding and of the contents of the honey pot, and that he found them both to contain a deadly poison, called corrosive sublimate of mercury, and that the symptoms exhibited by the Perigos' were consistent with the effects of this drug.

In her defence, Bateman claimed that she did not commit the crimes and tried to blame Miss Blythe. However, dozens of witnesses testified to Mary's criminal activities including fraud, extortion and abortion.

In his summing up, the Judge said that it was strange in a case of so much suspicion, that the body of Rebecca Perigo should have been buried without any inquiry as to the cause of death. He said that the main question was, did the prisoner contrive the means to induce the deceased to take it? If she did so contrive the means, the intent could only be to kill the intended victim.

The jury quickly returned a guilty verdict. The judge pronounced sentence and instructed that she would be hanged with the following words:

Mary Bateman, you have been convicted of wilful murder by a jury who, after having examined your case with caution, have, constrained by the force of evidence, pronounced you guilty. It only remains for me to fulfil my painful duty by passing upon you the awful sentence of the law. After you have been so long in the situation in which you now stand, and harassed as your mind must be by the long detail of your crimes and by listening to the sufferings you have occasioned, I do not wish to add to your distress by saying more than my duty renders necessary. Of your guilt, there cannot remain a particle of doubt in the breast of anyone who has heard your case. You entered into a long and premeditated system of fraud, which you carried on from a length of time which is most astonishing, and by means which one would have supposed could not, in this age and nation, have been practised with success.

To prevent a discovery of your complicated fraud, and the punishment which must have resulted therefrom, you deliberately contrived the death of the persons you had so grossly injured, and that by means of poison, a mode of destruction against which there is no sure protection. But your guilty design was not fully accomplished, and, after so extraordinary a lapse of time, you are reserved as a signal example of the justice of that mysterious Providence, which, sooner or later, overtakes guilt like yours.

At the very time when you were apprehended, there is the greatest reason to suppose, that if your surviving victim had met you alone, as you wished him to do, you would have administered to him a more deadly dose, which would have completed the diabolical project you had long before formed, but which at that time only partially succeeded; for upon your person, at that moment, was found a phial containing a most deadly poison.

For crimes like yours, in this world, the gates of mercy are closed. You afforded your victim no time for preparation, but the law, while it dooms you to death, has, in its mercy, afforded you time for repentance, and the assistance of pious and devout men, whose admonitions, and prayers, and counsels may assist to prepare you for another world, where even your crimes, if severely repented of, may find mercy.

Following the Judge's statement, the clerk of the arraigns said,

'Mary Bateman, what have you to say, why immediate execution should not be awarded against you?' She replied, to a stunned court, that she was twenty-two weeks pregnant. On this news the Judge ordered the sheriff to assemble a jury of matrons. Twelve married women were eventually brought together and were sworn in court to ascertain whether Bateman was telling the truth. They decided that she was not, and so Bateman was remanded back to prison.

During the brief interval between her receiving the death sentence and her execution, the Reverend George Brown made repeated attempts to try and get Bateman to acknowledge and confess her crimes, but didn't succeed and she retained her caution and mystery right to the end. Indeed, as if to prove that old habits die hard she could not resist temptation and swindled fellow prisoners with promises of reprieves.

On the day before her execution she wrote a letter to her husband, in which she enclosed her wedding-ring, with a request that it should be given to her daughter. She admitted that she had been guilty of many frauds, but still denied that she had had any intention to produce the death of William or Rebecca Perigo.

At five o'clock on the Monday morning, 20 March 1809, Mary Bateman was called from her cell to be executed. She received the communion with some other prisoners, but all final efforts to persuade her to confess to her crimes proved in vain. She kissed her youngest child and made her way to the gallows.

As she stood on the platform, silence fell upon the people who had gathered to witness the event. Reverend Brown again tried to get her to confess but Bateman stubbornly protested her innocence. Almost immediately the drop fell and Mary Bateman, 'The Yorkshire Witch' was dead.

Her body remained suspended during the usual time, was cut down, and sent to the General Infirmary at Leeds to be anatomized. Large crowds met the hearse which arrived at the infirmary at about midnight. A total of £30 was raised by people paying 3d to see the body. Dr William Hey was responsible for the public dissection of her body and people paid up to half a guinea to watch him at work with over fifty women attending his lecture on the eye. Bateman was one of the first criminals to be

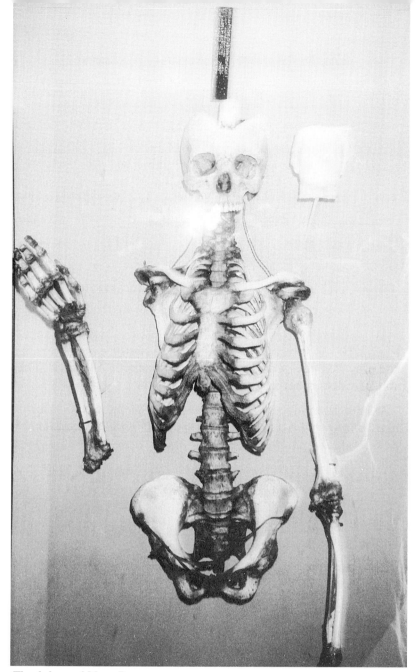

The skeleton of Mary Bateman.. Thackray Medical Museum, Leeds

anatomized in the thirst for medical knowledge, which was great in the early nineteenth century.

The last dying words of Bateman were published along with those of Joseph Brown who was executed at York Castle on the

The Laſt Dying Words, Speech, and Confeſſion of JOSEPH BROWN and MAR
BATEMAN, who were executed at the Drop behind the Caſtle of York, on Monday th
20th of March, 1809, BROWN for the wilful Murder of Mrs. Elizabeth Fletcher—an
BATEMAN for the wilful Murder of Rebecca Perrigo.

Portion of the copy of the last words, speech and confession of Mary Bateman. York
Castle Museum

same day for the wilful murder of Elizabeth Fletcher. The
published document read:

> *Mary Bateman, aged 41, who now forfeits her life for Witchcraft
> and Murder, practised with every aggravation that exhortation,
> protracted, and painful death could invent; accompanied by the
> most unprecedented instances of credulity that ever engaged public
> attention.*

Chapter 9

Murder in Batley
1865

Sarah Brooke was a sixty-year-old widow and her eighteen-year-old daughter Hannah, who was a mill-hand, lived with her in Hulme Street, Batley. Until August 1865, Eli Sykes, aged nineteen and a cloth finisher, also from Batley had been going out with Hannah. The couple met on 10 March 1863 as the town, along with the rest of the country, was celebrating the marriage of the Prince and Princess of Wales. The two of them were frequently seen together and everyone assumed they would eventually get married. The relationship between Sykes and Brooke was very affectionate and though the girl had quite often 'scolded' Sykes, there was never any hint that the relationship was in trouble.

However, at a Dewsbury feast in the July of 1865, Hannah Brooke met a young man from Wakefield called James Hurst and a relationship grew between them. Her feelings for Sykes cooled rapidly and she hinted that his 'attendance was no longer desirable'.

On Sunday 13 August, Hannah Brooke was having tea with Hurst at his house and, at about five o'clock, the two were at the front door when Sykes walked by. He returned at about ten o'clock and this time knocked on the door to be told by Hurst that Hannah had gone home. Striking his hat violently against the door, Sykes said: 'If I cannot have her, no one else shall.' Hurst answered: 'Eli, I think you're going out of your mind' to which Sykes responded: 'you'll see'.

Sykes had also begun to follow Hannah Brooke; waiting for her at the houses of friends she visited. He told people that if he could not have her nobody else would and he said he was 'wound up to a fearful pitch of passion' by her jeering when he again professed his love.

Sykes was a private in No 3 (Batley Carr) company of the 29th (Dewsbury) West York Volunteer Corps, and paraded with his corps on Saturday, 19 August between three and four o'clock in the afternoon. The men were formed into three companies and were marched into Batley. After waiting at the station they went to Drighlington by the West Yorkshire line and were joined at Drighlington by the Birstal corps before having battalion drill.

The men returned to Batley station at about twenty to ten in the evening and by ten-thirty Sykes was with a friend, William Bentley Walton in Batley Station. He was still dressed in his volunteer uniform with a gun in his hand and a bayonet on top of it. Walton knew of the problems there had been between Sykes and Hannah Brooke since Hurst came on the scene and when Sykes said he was going round to the Brooke household, he strongly advised him not to go.

Sykes left Batley Station with a couple of friends from the battalion. He asked one of them if they would walk with him into Batley but the friend declined as it was late. Sykes then turned up the hill into town and was later seen in Commercial Street.

Ignoring his friend's advice Sykes went to the Brooke's house and asked Hannah if she still wanted a relationship with him. She said no and the two had a furious row before Sykes forced himself into the house. Hannah fled into the living room but he followed her and started attacking her with the butt end of his rifle.

Sarah Brooke witnessed the attack and rushed to try and help her daughter, but this made Sykes more determined and he drew his bayonet, stabbing both women repeatedly. Sarah, though she had multiple wounds, managed to reach the door to cry for help.

It was about eleven o'clock on the Saturday night and Joseph Pease, a neighbour of Sarah Brooke heard her scream out 'murder' three or four times. He rushed round to the house and found Hannah bleeding heavily from the neck and the body. Sykes was just a few feet away from her and was using his bayonet to stab at his throat. The rifle was laid on the floor and the stock was broken. Pease grabbed Sykes and threw him down to the floor. The two men fought and in the process of trying to disarm Sykes, Pease was stabbed in the side. Sarah followed the men into the room, but soon after, she stumbled and fell to the ground. Pease saw that her nightdress was stained with blood, and she soon died.

After Pease entered the house, others were alerted by the screams and shouts coming from the house; Sykes was overcome and the bayonet, dripping with blood, removed from his hand. Police and medical assistance was soon on hand and Sergeant English formally charged Sykes with the murder of Sarah and Hannah Brooke. Sykes took a look at the corpses laid on the bed, threw his head back but made no remark. When additional policemen came to the scene, Sykes was quickly taken to the lock-ups in Dewsbury and, even though it was late in the evening, crowds

DOUBLE MURDER AT BATLEY
BY A
VOLUNTEER RIFLEMAN.
ATTEMPTED SUICIDE OF THE MURDERER.

A crime of almost unexampled atrocity in this district was committed on Saturday night, at Batley, where a young man named Eli Sykes murdered his sweetheart, Hannah Brooke, and her mother, Sarah Brooke, and afterwards made a determined attempt upon his own existence. Sykes, who is a cloth finisher by trade, is only nineteen years of age, and his victims were aged respectively eighteen and sixty. The double murder of which the young man stands charged appears to have been prompted by deep-rooted feelings of jealousy ; and the details reveal in a most impressive manner the awful results of evil passion ungoverned by reason. The acquaintance of Hannah Brooke with her murderer appears to have commenced on the 10th of March, 1863. They met each other on the occasion when Batley, along with the rest of the country, was celebrating the marriage of the Prince and Princess of Wales, and the friendship then begun ripened into affection. A quarrel took place some months after, but this was made up in a short time. At the Dewsbury fair, in October last, the parties met together on apparently amicable and loving terms. From that time until July last, Sykes called frequently at the house of the ill-fated women who have met their death by his hands. Hannah and he were seen frequently together, and it was generally considered that their intimacy would in process of time lead to a marriage. At the Dewsbury feast, however, in July last, Hannah Brooke seems to have met with a young man from Wakefield, whose attractions proved irresistible, and many hints were from this time thrown out to Sykes

Headline noting 'Double Murder at Batley'. Bradford Observer

began to gather at the front of the house as news of the double murder spread.

Sykes had caused wounds to his neck in five places, though none of these were serious injuries and he was taken into custody. On the way to prison, Police constable Murray told him that he did not have to say anything as anything he did say could be given in evidence against him. However, Sykes rose on his arm and made the following statement:

I feel easier in my mind, and better satisfied now than before I did it. I was with Hannah Brooke last Monday night and we were on good terms. I went on Saturday night, between ten and eleven o'clock, and her and her mother began calling me, and telling me to go away, they did not want me there. I asked Hannah if she'd ever go with me again, and she said 'no'. I asked her if she wasn't going with another man from Wakefield, and she said 'yes'. Hannah sat down on a chair and began singing, and it aggravated me. I struck her with the butt end of my gun, and she

Batley Police Station. The author

cried out 'Oh Eli, let me alone and I'll go with you', but I pulled
my bayonet out of my sheath and ran it into her. Her mother got
up out of bed and tried to prevent me, and I ran my bayonet into
her. Although I murdered her I loved her – I have told her many
a time I'd have my revenge, and I've got it now.

Sykes also said that he had asked Hannah if she was seeing someone else and she admitted that she was. On questioning, Sykes denied that he was drunk when committing the attack, but after making the statement he was breathing heavily and spitting blood.

Sykes faced examination before Leeds Magistrates where he was formally charged with the wilful murder of Sarah Brooke and Hannah Brooke in Batley on 19 August. He was present in court and was described the next day as a tall, raw boned youth with a coarse face and wild looking eyes. He appeared in plain clothes as some of his colleagues on the rifle corps helped him to exchange the bloodstained uniform, which he had worn on the Saturday night for the 'ordinary dress of a civilian'.

There was great shock in Batley and the greater Leeds area as news spread of the double murder. The shock was even greater to those who knew Hannah and Sarah Brooke and also those who had come into contact with Eli Sykes. He generally had a good reputation among his peers and his workmates spoke of his good character, his steadiness at drill, his great civility and good behaviour.

On the Sunday, the day after the attacks took place, Sykes had several visitors in prison and seemed in very good heart despite the horror of the previous evening. He had visits from his father, brother and sister and, around the prison was seen laughing and whistling. When awoken on the Sunday morning, Sykes said he 'felt comfortable and happy' and when asked if he wanted anything, replied 'something to sup'.

The inquest into the deaths was heard in Batley on the Monday morning. The post-mortem examination on the body of Hannah Brooke had found seven incised wounds upon her body, one of which would have proved fatal. Sykes had stabbed Sarah Brooke nine times.

The neighbour, Joseph Pease, giving evidence, said that at

about eleven o'clock he heard Sarah Brooke shout 'murder' and yell 'He is murdering our Hannah in the house'. Pease ran into the house and saw Sykes stabbing himself in the neck with the bayonet. Peace stopped him and, along with a man called William Fawcett managed to hold Sykes down until the police arrived.

When the police got to the house they saw that Sykes was suffering from self-inflicted wounds to the throat. Hannah had managed to get to her feet, but had blood pouring from her mouth; she collapsed in the arms of someone and was put on a bed. Sarah Brooke was also bleeding when she came into the room and she also collapsed onto the floor. It appeared from the evidence that Sarah Brooke died first with Hannah following a little while later.

Sergeant Thomas English told the inquest that when he arrived the house was full of people with crowds outside the door. The prisoner was being held down and was bleeding from five small stab wounds in his neck. He tried to lift Sykes into a chair, but the prisoner took this as his cue to try and escape and English was forced to handcuff him. The officer said that when he arrived Sarah Brooke was still alive but was bleeding from wounds to her neck and she died in a few minutes. Hannah was also lying on a bed and was bleeding from wounds to her mouth and neck. Some people were trying to give her some water and she responded, trying to speak but she was unable to do so and died almost immediately.

Another witness, George Fernley Brooke, was Sarah Brooke's son and Hannah's brother. He knew Sykes and met him in Dewsbury after he and Hannah had split up. Sykes had said that he was so upset by the parting that he did not know what to do. Brooke had tried to reassure him by saying that there were plenty more women out there for him.

On the following Tuesday, Batley churchyard witnessed the funerals of Sarah and Hannah Brooke. Trains calling into Batley Station that day were full of people wanting to see the spectacle, witness to the publicity the case had attracted in the West Yorkshire region. It was estimated that about 20,000 people flocked to line the route that the cortège took.

Eli Sykes was committed for trial at the West Yorkshire Assizes

Batley churchyard. The author

where his defence team told the jury that the accused was a mere boy, only nineteen, who was quiet and inoffensive. Mr Foster argued that Hannah Brooke had taunted Sykes over the fact that she was now seeing someone else and that jealousy had been the factor which had driven Sykes to commit the 'dreadful act'. He asked the jury that, because of the multiple stabbings of the two women, the fact that he also tried to stab Peace and had also stabbed himself in the throat, they should consider that Sykes had lost control for a time and that they should convict Sykes of the lesser offence of manslaughter.

Foster added that the defendant had committed the acts because of 'a sudden transport of passion brought on by the girl'. He argued that the jealousy felt by Sykes differed greatly to the black resolution to commit murder. He said that if Sykes had intended to murder his victims he would have taken great care not to discharge his rifle when he was with the Volunteer Corps in the afternoon. The fact that he stabbed Hannah, her mother, himself and then Peace who tried to intervene, indicated that he was out of control and did not have malice aforethought.

He said that Sykes 'had been angered like a wild beast by the exasperating conduct of her from whom he least expected it'. For the prosecution, Mr Middleton made much of the fact that Sykes had said that if he could not have Hannah Brooke no one else could. He also stressed that whilst the blood of the two women was still 'red upon his hands' Sykes had told the surgeon and police that he had felt easier than he had for a fortnight.

The jury, after having retired for twenty-five minutes, returned with a verdict of 'Guilty'. Sykes immediately raised his clasped hands above his head and his lips moved silently, as if in secret prayer. He then addressed the court, saying:

What have I done, I never had it in my mind to do in my life before it was done. She provoked me to do what I have done, and began singing 'You may go to the devil for me'. Many an hour have I cried with her, and she told me many and many a time that she was going with him [her Wakefield lover]*; but still I kept trying to gain her affections, I had never struck her before. I hope I shall meet her in heaven.*

Sykes then broke down in floods of tears and sank to his knees. The judge appeared deeply affected, but put on the black cap and said:

Eli Sykes, you have been found guilty of the crime of wilful murder, and it is my duty to pass upon you the sentence of the law. And I would do that at once only that one's feelings revolt in consigning a fellow creature to death, at not saying a word of interest, comfort or consolation.

I am glad to have heard the expressions of religious feeling which have fallen from your lips. Your young life up to the commission of this grievous crime cannot have been very guilty; and assuredly if you seek for mercy from above by prayer and by repentance, that mercy will be obtained. Let me then implore you not for one moment, during the short time you have to live, to harden your heart. Do your best to prepare yourself for the awful change that awaits you; and do not suppose among the multitudes of those good men who will hear of your sentence, which they will believe to be just, there will not be many among them who between this and your last hour will pray to Almighty God with all their hearts that he may be merciful to you.

After his conviction Sykes was placed in a cell at Armley Gaol which had been occupied by James Sargisson the notorious murderer who was executed in 1864. It was a corner cell on the first floor of the prison and was used as the condemned cell as it was larger than others.

One evening the prison chaplain saw Sykes with a warder also in attendance. The chaplain left at about six-thirty but the door was left slightly open and Sykes saw this as his opportunity to hasten his inevitable death. He rushed past the warder, ran up the stairs to the second landing and threw himself about twenty-five feet to the floor below.

The officer in charge rushed to his side and found him lying unconscious and with assistance took him back to his cell where he was seen by the prison surgeon Mr Price. He quickly regained consciousness but it was soon clear that he had been seriously injured.

Both of his legs were badly broken in the fall and his skull was fractured; he was bleeding profusely from his left leg and

The interior of Armley Gaol. West Yorkshire Archive Service

A cartoon of prisoners in Armley Gaol, during the nineteenth century. West Yorkshire
Archive Service.

forehead. Though fully conscious by this time, he was
incoherent, calling out 'she's before me, she's before me. Take
her away!' His condition deteriorated and an examination
revealed that he had suffered a secondary haemorrhage of the
wound in his foot. The loss of blood left him in a very weak

THE CONVICT ELI SYKES ATTEMPTING TO COMMIT SUICIDE.—On Sunday evening, the convict Eli Sykes made an attempt, after the fashion of Victor Townley, to commit suicide in Armley Gaol. The chaplain of the prison, after an interview with him, had left the door of his cell open. The prisoner took advantage of this, and suddenly rushed out in spite of the efforts of a turnkey to restrain him. He passed rapidly up the corridor, ascended the stairs to the uppermost balcony, and threw himself headlong into the area below. The following are additional particulars :—The prisoner, after his conviction, was placed in the cell which was occupied by Sargisson. This is a corner cell on the first storey, and is appropriated as the condemned cell because of its being somewhat larger than the others. The rule adopted by the governor, in such cases, is to place in the cell with the condemned prisoner a warder. The cell is double locked from the outside, and it is the duty of any person leaving it to see that the door is properly secured. On Saturday evening the chaplain of the gaol, in the discharge of his solemn duty to the condemned man, visited Sykes, and during his visit the warder also continued in charge. The rev. gentleman retired from the cell about half-past six o'clock. By some inadvertence the door was left slightly open, and Sykes, who seems to have been ready to avail himself of the first opportunity which presented itself of escaping from a public death, rushed past the warder, ran up the second landing, and deliberately threw himself over the balustrades to the floor beneath—the fall being about 25 or 26 feet. He alighted on his feet, and then fell head foremost to the floor. The officer in charge having recovered from the surprise which the conduct of Sykes had produced, ran to his assistance and found him lying insensible. He was taken up and again conveyed to his cell, and Mr. Price, the surgeon of the gaol, and subsequently Mr. Wheelhouse, were called in. Sykes regained consciousness in about half an hour, and although seriously injured, he is not in a hopeless condition.

An article on Eli Sykes' suicide attempt.
Leeds Mercury

condition, though he was still determined to take his own life and several times he tried to tear off his bandages to re-open the wounds.

Mr Price the prison surgeon succeeded briefly in stopping the bleeding and Sykes rallied briefly; he began speaking to the warders. However, at about nine in the evening the bleeding continued and Sykes soon died from loss of blood.

At the inquest the jury returned a verdict of *felo de se* and Sykes was buried within the precincts of the prison.

Chapter 10

The Resurrectionists
1826-1831

The resurrectionists or 'bodysnatchers' arose from the advance in surgery in the nineteenth century and the resulting greater need for anatomical study. Surgeons were no longer crude butchers and a thorough understanding of anatomy was a prerequisite for safe and effective operative techniques. Surgeons had limited access to bodies, mainly hanged criminals, so the demand for bodies to work on well exceeded the supply.

Against this background, medical ethics played little part in anatomy. Some teachers purchased bodies from London where gangs of 'resurrectionists' made a precarious living by robbing graves. They transported cadavers in sacks or barrels disguised as merchandise. This more than once caused trouble when tradesmen mistakenly opened consignments. Other teachers managed to 'procure' bodies locally and students were sometimes even expected to provide specimens for themselves. This frequently led to body snatching and their nocturnal activity often aroused public animosity.

These men in the eighteenth and early nineteenth centuries worked at night, digging up freshly interred bodies for sale to surgeons and medical schools. Many were rough types who engaged in all manner of dishonest dealing. Others were comparatively reliable men who probably felt justified that theirs was a legitimate but difficult business supplying 'a branch of scientific goods'.

Their method of working was an acquired skill. To avoid detection they left a grave with little trace of interference, carefully replacing such things as flower vases. They did not open the whole grave but dug a small hole through which they contrived to haul the body by means of a rope, taking no part of the coffin or shroud.

Cartoon showing bodysnatchers at work. Thackray Medical Museum

Legally there was no property value in a corpse and magistrates would often refuse to convict them on the grounds of merely opening graves. In time, various by-laws were designed to combat this nuisance. The first was the Select Committee Enquiry of 1828, which was entitled 'A Bill to prevent unlawful disinterment and to regulate schools of anatomy'. Also a Select Committee to 'enquire into the manner of obtaining subjects for dissection by schools of Anatomy and the State of Law affecting persons employed in obtaining and dissecting bodies' was appointed.

Public feeling, now strongly in favour of some change in the law, was greatly intensified by some horrible murders perpetrated in London by three men, Bishop, Williams and May. Their ultimate atrocity was the murder of a fourteen-year-old boy whose body they tried to sell at Guys Hospital for twelve guineas. When refused, they moved on to Kings College where a demonstrator became suspicious and called the police. This incident did much to accelerate the progress of the *Anatomy Bill*, which finally became law on 1 August 1832.

In Leeds, a combination of the heavy industry with poor working conditions, inadequate housing with poor hygiene and the intense pollution of the air all contributed to a very high death rate which rose rapidly with the population increase.

New cemeteries sprang up which became the targets for a highly organised group of 'resurrectionists'. There were a number of cases of bodysnatching in the region and the practice was so prevalent in some areas of Leeds that the communities organised societies (Grave Clubs) to cater for the relatives of the deceased persons and to devise measures to beat the body snatchers. These measures included guarding newly buried bodies for five weeks and burying corpses twelve feet down with iron staves set into the earth at fixed intervals immediately above the coffin.

Robert Baker was a Leeds surgeon who thrived on teaching anatomy to his pupils. A newly qualified Leeds surgeon keen to further his career, his name was synonymous with some of the more notorious cases of bodysnatching in Leeds during the nineteenth century.

Liaising with some men who were keen to supply him with dead bodies, for a price, the surgeon paid them four pounds, a month's wages for a labourer, to dig up a body from a nearby graveyard. The body was duly delivered but the deceased's family visited the grave the following day and noticed it missing. This prompted a poster campaign calling for the return of the body. Baker panicked and disguised the body by coiling it into a square box. He then rushed the package to an inn on the edge of Leeds from where it was to be taken to Edinburgh and, he

South Parade. Twelve bodies were dissected in Charles Turner Thackrah's house here.
The author

assumed that it would not be traced back.

However, en route through York, the authorities became suspicious of the box and with the police called, it was discovered to contain the body of Martha Oddy. Two men, Cox and Armstrong, were caught and evidence also linked Baker with the crimes.

Cox went to court in 1826 in a separate case, for disinterring the body of Thomas Daniels for the purpose of dissection. Daniels, who worked as a joiner in Leeds, died on 30 December 1825 and was buried in St John's churchyard on 1 January 1926. Daniels' son became suspicious due to a report in newspapers of a dead body having been found in Newcastle en route from Leeds. He was successful in having the tomb opened and found the coffin to be empty. He then went up to Newcastle, and, having had the body disinterred, found it to be his father. It was placed in a lead coffin and was then buried in the churchyard back in Leeds.

Cox was in possession of the body on 5 January when he brought it in a box, covered with matting to the hotel coach office from where it was forwarded on to Newcastle. At his trial the judge said that it could be argued on the part of the defence, that it was necessary for the purposes of medical science that surgeons should have the means of dissection, and have the

Newspaper article on the resurrectionists. Leeds Mercury

SUSPICION OF MURDER FOR ANATOMICAL PURPOSES

A good deal of excitement has prevailed in this town during the last week, in consequence of the seizure of a dead body destined for some anatomical purpose, under circumstances which excited a suspicion that it had been obtained by a much more heinous crime than that of violating the sanctuary of the tomb. We shall merely state such facts as have been given in evidence, without a single sentence by way of comment.

On Monday evening last, about eight o'clock, a box was about to be placed upon the Courier coach, which goes to Carlisle, when the attention of a police officer was called to it. The box was opened, and found to contain the body of a young man. This led to the apprehension of several individuals.—The body was taken to the Court House; the magistrates issued a placard, describing the body and the circumstances under which it had been detained, and stating that it would be at the Court-House for inspection. It was there seen by several thousand people, but no one identified it. On Thursday afternoon, in consequence of suspicions being entertained that the deceased had come by his death in an unfair manner, the Coroner issued his warrant for holding an inquest, preparatory to which the body was removed to the Infirmary, where a post mortem examination took place. At four o'clock in the afternoon of Thursday, the Coroner, Robert Barr, Esq., assembled a jury at the Griffin Inn: after they were sworn, they repaired to the Infirmary, to view the body, and on their return the following witnesses were examined :—

Wm. Hatton is one of the constables of Leeds; he stated that

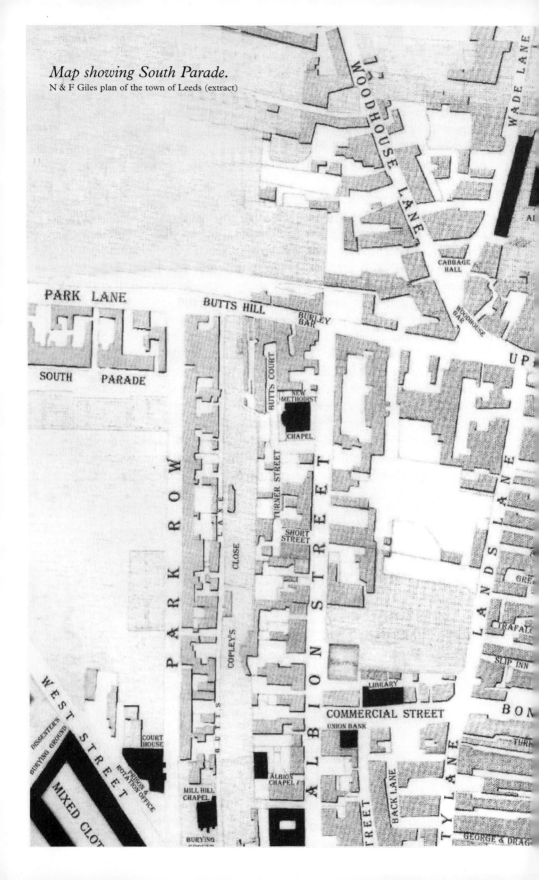

Map showing South Parade.
N & F Giles plan of the town of Leeds (extract)

opportunity of examining dead bodies, and that it was much better that they should attain this knowledge by operating upon inanimate rather than upon living bodies. The judge added that he had sympathy for this view but that the jury was there to consider the law rather than the morals of the case. Cox was found guilty by the jury and was imprisoned in York Castle for six months.

Baker was implicated in the trial of Armstrong case in which the grave was left entirely open after the body had been removed, with the shroud, linen and other items left scattered around the churchyard. Martha Oddy died on 7 March and was buried three days later in Armley chapel yard. On the following Monday, the grave was found to have been opened and the body had been removed. After some information from the police, Martha's uncle accompanied the Chief Constable Edward Read to the *Black Swan* in York. There they found a box, which, when opened, contained the body of Martha.

William Broadbent, a grave-digger at Armley at the time said that Thomas Smith, who had been named as an accomplice of Armstrong, was in the churchyard at the time and he had asked Broadbent about the depth of the grave. William Thompson, giving evidence, remembered a conversation he had with Armstrong on Saturday, 11 March in which Armstrong had offered him a guinea if he would go with him to Armley churchyard and help him to get a body.

In the dock, Robert Baker admitted that he knew Armstrong and had seen him on 11 March when he had been told that Armstrong had a body and was willing to sell it to Baker. The surgeon refused, but later relented and agreed to buy it. The following Monday, Baker met with Armstrong and another man who had a sack containing the body. They gave the sack to Baker who took it in a gig to the *Cross-Roads Inn*.

In court Cox asked Baker why he wanted the body and he replied: 'For the purpose of dissection'. Cox said: 'No, you wanted to export and make a profit of it' but Baker stressed that was not his intention.

Mr Maude, for the prosecution, said that this case was similar to the original case involving Cox but caused even greater aggravation to those involved. He said it must excite the indignation of even those medical men whom:

> *Might be most disposed to connive at practices of this kind, for the body had been removed with that brutal disregard to the feelings of relatives, which of itself merited the severest punishment.*

The jury found Armstrong guilty and he was sentenced by the recorder to six months imprisonment in York Castle. The recorder, Mr Hardy, in passing sentence on Cox and Armstrong observed that:

> *Whatever allowance might be made for medical men, who sought by the examination of dead bodies to obtain knowledge useful to society, no such palliation applied to the cases of prisoners who had been influenced by the mere love of filthy lucre.*

Baker was acquitted as his intention to 'promote knowledge' supposedly negated culpability. However, his career prospects suffered as a result of his 'business venture' and he found it hard to obtain work after the trial.

Over five years later, on 11 December 1831, the resurrectionists were back at work and the *Leeds Mercury* reported on one particular case:

> *A good deal of excitement has prevailed in this town during the last week, in consequence of the seizure of a dead body, destined for some anatomical purpose, under circumstances which excited a suspicion that it had been obtained by a much more heinous crime than that of violating the sanctuary of the tomb.*

John Hodgson was a specialist in providing bodies for 'medical gentlemen' and he was accused of stealing the dead body of Thomas Rothery from the burial ground of the Episcopal Chapel, Wortley in January 1831. The body of Rothery, a dyer, whose death was caused by falling into a dye-pan filled with heated liquor at a Dye-house, was buried on Sunday, 5 January and was stolen on the following Thursday.

A warrant was issued for the arrest of Hodgson, but he had disappeared before Edward Read, the Chief Constable, apprehended him in Harrogate. At his trial Hodgson managed to persuade some dignified medical people to speak to the jury about the importance of dissection to medical research.

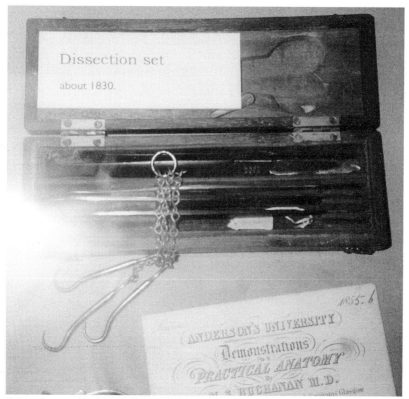

Dissection set dated from about 1830. Thackray Medical Museum

Hodgson told the court:

> *I was connected with a medical man in the taking of this body and it was for the purpose of mutually dissecting it. I could not give up his name without utterly ruining him, and if you send me to prison you will ruin my prospects for life.*

The Judge said that he sympathised with the scientific research aspect of the case but he had a duty to protect the rights of the dead man's relatives. However, he felt that he could be lenient and sentenced Hodgson to six weeks in York Castle.

Hodgson was not long out of prison before he reverted to his old trade and in November 1831 he was part of a gang rounded up when police seized a suspicious package that was being placed on the carrier coach at the *Rose and Crown Inn*, Leeds.

Rose and Crown Yard showing the Rose & Crown Inn *where the bodies were traced back to.* The Thoresby Society

Henry Teale had first met Hodgson at the annual Chapeltown feast event. The two became friends and Hodgson told him of his 'job'. Teale soon became part of the gang along with two other men, John Pickering and John Wood. He was given a list of graveyards including East Ardsley and told that two bodies were needed. Teale ordered two gigs for the night of 2 November.

On that night the four men went to the graveyard and began digging. They soon came across a small coffin and quickly removed the lid, took out the body, stripped off the linen and put it in a sack. The linen was put back into the grave which was then filled in. The gang later found a larger body, which they put into another sack;

they put the bodies onto gigs and drove back to Leeds.

The two bodies were taken to Norman's Yard House off Woodhouse Lane where they were prepared for their journey. The small body went by coach to a surgeon in Edinburgh, but the bigger body took much longer to prepare and the gang missed the coach. As a result it was taken on a gig to Pickering's house in Tobacco Mill Lane and it was as the gang tried to move the body to Rose and Crown Yard that they were spotted and suspicions were aroused.

William Penistone kept a public house in the Little London area of Leeds, and also owned a house in Tobacco Mill Lane, Sheepscar. He had let the house to Pickering but then entered into negotiation with somebody else who wished to buy the property. Mrs Evans, the wife of the man who wanted to buy the house and Penistone entered the house to look around before

Rose and Crown Yard. The Thoresby Society

Ship Yard as it appeared at the turn of the century. One of the resurrectionists was arrested here. The Thoresby Society

the sale and noticed that one of the cupboards was locked.

They went to a public house called the *Bold Dragon* to wait for Pickering to get home and Penistone recognised a young man who came in for a light. He was a man who had been seen with Pickering in the house a few days earlier, so they followed him to the house and waited. They soon heard noises as if several people were walking about in the house near the door. They heard the door open and saw a handcart come out with a box upon it. There were three men with the cart and they headed towards Leeds taking the box to the Crown Coach Office.

Penistone took the opportunity to go back into the house and saw that the door of the cupboard which had been locked on his last visit, had been broken into small pieces. He also noticed some bloodstains on the floor.

He called the police who traced the box to the *Rose and*

Ship Yard as it appears today. The author

Bond Street. John Pickering's home was here. The author

Crown Inn. Destined for Carlisle, it was found to contain the body of a young man, thought to be in his early twenties, five feet three inches high with brown hair and blue eyes. He was later identified as Robert Hudson who hanged himself in the cabin of a coalpit at East Ardsley and was buried in the local churchyard.

Two cards were on top of the box, one addressed to Carlisle and the other to a Benjamin Thompson of Edinburgh. PC William Halton went to the schoolroom of John Pickering in Bond Street where he found Pickering, his wife and John Hodgson. Pickering and Hodgson were taken into custody.

Constable Halton returned to the house in Tobacco Mill Lane and found a sack, which contained a spade, a brace, a gimblet, and another sack covered in blood. There was also a carpetbag close to the sack, which contained a short spade, a pair of overalls, a knife and an iron instrument used for breaking open coffins.

At the trial Thomas Chorley, a surgeon at the Leeds Infirmary, said that he saw the body of the dead man at the Infirmary and his attention was drawn to marks on the throat and on each side of the neck. He also noticed that the inner membrane of the windpipe was of an unusually dark colour. External pressure on the neck was calculated to produce the appearances in the windpipe which he had described and he thought the injuries were consistent with the victim having been strangled.

He said that the body had no appearance of ever having been buried, as it did not appear to have been washed. He thought that the dead man must have been deceased for about ten days to a fortnight and that he was between eighteen and twenty years of age.

John Hodgson himself questioned Thomas Chorley and put forward the opinion that the body had been so decomposed that it was impossible to put forward any argument as to the cause of death. This was denied by Mr Chorley who stood by his verdict, that the person had died through strangulation.

Jonathan Bedford, the sexton at East Ardsley church, said that he was called upon to open the grave and before he got to the bottom, he found some linen. The coffin had been disturbed and the body had gone. Inside the coffin were an iron bludgeon and a glove and holes had been bored into the lid of the coffin to admit a saw with a piece of the coffin having been sawn away.

In April 1832 Teale retold his story in court and because he had turned King's Evidence he was discharged. The rest of the gang were not as lucky. Hodgson, clearly marked as the ringleader, was sentenced to one year's imprisonment with the others receiving sentences of three months imprisonment.

Leeds was certainly not the only city to be affected by the resurrectionists and Edinburgh was the scene of one of the most notorious tales. Dr Robert Knox, a prominent anatomist paid two Irishmen, William Burke and William Hare £10 a body to help fuel their drinking habits. Knox believed that the pair were digging up bodies from local graveyards when they were actually luring guests from their lodgings and plying them with alcohol until they were dunked head first into a beer barrel filled with water and held there until he or she drowned.

The pair then stashed the bodies in their cellar before passing them on to Knox. There were no signs of violence upon the bodies so Knox had no idea of the murders. After sixteen people had been killed in this way, thirteen of whom had been passed on to Knox, suspicions were aroused and the police raided Hare's lodgings where they uncovered a corpse beneath some hay. Knox was soon implicated.

At the trial Burke was granted immunity if he testified against Hare. He did and Hare suffered the death penalty, while Burke fled upon his acquittal. However, Knox was also a victim and he certainly suffered through his part in the crimes as his reputation never recovered.

The cases in Leeds, Edinburgh and other cities, notably London, led to a nationwide debate on a possible change in the law regarding research on bodies. The government fought shy of this but eventually, the *Anatomy Act* of 1832 was formed. It allowed bodies of the poor to be taken from hospitals and workhouses for use in teaching.

Chapter 11

The Roundhay Murder
1859

At about about five o'clock on the Saturday evening of 6 August 1859, Richard Broughton, aged sixty-seven, who lived in Rose Cottage Yard, Roundhay, set off from his home in the direction of the centre of Leeds. He often went for a stroll, being an active man and intended to have a long walk on a balmy late summer evening. Carrying a florin in his pocket, and a German silver watch he walked along Horse Shoe Lane and then took a footpath, leading from Seacroft to Leeds. He had reached the top of an oat field, Ox Pasture, near to Harehills Lane when he was attacked by two men, one of whom was carrying a bludgeon. Broughton fell into a hedge, but the two attackers continued to rein blows upon his body, causing five wounds in particular to his skull, one causing it to fracture. The two men may have then been disturbed as the man's watch was taken though his florin was left untouched.

Broughton regained consciousness and staggered to his feet. Several people saw him as he tried to pick himself up and carry on with his journey. A group of men saw him trying to make his way down the street, as if drunk, but they noticed that blood was streaming down his face. When they found out that he lived in Roundhay, they insisted on him going back there, rather than continuing to walk towards Leeds and they offered to walk with him. However, though in a terrible state and barely coherent, he insisted on getting home himself. On his way back home, passing the scene of the attack, he met a man called Walter Barber. By this time Broughton was bleeding from his head and his clothes were also covered in blood. He took off his hat and Barber noticed that there were five wounds on his head. Broughton pointed to them and managed to murmur the words, 'two men'.

Headline concerning the 'murder of an old man near Leeds'. Bradford Observer

Barber asked Broughton if he was able to walk home unaided, and again he insisted that he could. When he got home, in a terrible state, he was washed and tended to by his wife and neighbours and the surgeon, Mr Hey, was called. According to one witness, Broughton looked as if he had had a bucket of blood poured over him.

One neighbour, Thos Barber seeing that Broughton would not be conscious for long, asked him how it had happened. Broughton replied:

> By two men. One of them went up the hill slowly before me, till he got to the top of the hill, and there another man joined him. Then one of them struck me twice over the head, but before I became insensible I saw them go away in this direction [pointing towards York Road].

The only other detail Broughton was able to give was that one of his attackers was a young man, whilst the other was quite a bit older. He gradually deteriorated and Richard Broughton eventually died at about two o'clock on the Sunday morning.

When police made their way to the scene of the attack, they were able to find it with great ease. A hawthorn bush was beaten down and broken due to Broughton falling down on it. Traces of Broughton's hair and skin were found on some of the branches and a pool of blood could be seen underneath. A nearby stile was also covered in blood.

Such an apparently motiveless attack shocked the people of Leeds and in the immediate aftermath of the murder, the mayor of Leeds announced a £50 reward for information leading to the arrest of those responsible.

Police were desperate to make a quick arrest due to the

publicity the case had attracted, however, they had no leads and were struggling in the search for the culprits. Finally, two men were arrested and were brought up before Leeds Magistrates at the Town Hall. Walter Bearder, alias Smith and William Appleby were both aged about twenty-eight and were reported to be men of 'bad character'. At the time of their arrest, both men were at the House of Correction in Wakefield, due to a burglary in Batley, which had been committed just before Broughton's murder. Police suspected the pair of being responsible for both crimes and they were brought before Leeds magistrates under the writ of *habeas corpus*, though all the evidence was circumstantial.

Several witnesses came forward to say that the two men were very similar to those who were seen loitering near to the place where the murder was committed; the men were seen there a few minutes before the attack had taken place. However, none of the witnesses could be certain that Bearder and Appleby were the men they had seen on that day.

The watch which had been stolen from Broughton had then been taken to the pawnshop of a Mr Barrass in Dyer Street on the Saturday evening. The pawnbroker's assistant, in the shop at the time, believed that Bearder was the man who came in to the shop, but again was far from certain.

During examinations, a hedgestake was produced, which contained some blood and samples of hair and a witness was able to identify the weapon as one that he saw in the hands of a man near to where the murder took place. The weapon was eventually picked up about eighteen yards from the spot.

It was also revealed in court that between six and seven o'clock on the Saturday evening, about an hour and a half after the murder had been committed, Bearder and a man called John Dodd went to the house of a woman known as Shields who lived in Hargrave Court, Little Queen Street in Leeds. Bearder was seen coming out of the house into a yard with a basin which he filled with tap water before going back into the house. He went out into the yard once more, again to fill up the basin.

Shields was committed for trial for receiving stolen goods supposedly taken in the Batley burglary for which Bearder and Appleby had been charged. A pair of trousers and a coat were removed from the house and were taken possession of by the police. The trousers aroused particular suspicion, as they appeared to have spots of blood on them. On the same knee as the blood were some hairs and the other leg of the trousers was covered in dirt.

The trousers belonged to a man called Wilsher who lived in the same yard as Shields. He knew the two men who were suspected of both the burglary and the murder and said that Bearder had worn the pair of trousers on the day of the murder.

However, the evidence against both men did not look strong enough to the police and they were concerned that they did not have enough evidence which to charge Bearder or Appleby with murder. They were remanded in custody due to their part in the Batley burglary, but the Roundhay murder case took a new twist when nineteen-year-old Charles Normington was arrested in Sheffield in early September, a month after the murder had been committed.

The previous Saturday a man known as James Smales, a collier at a pit near Wakefield, went to Leeds to visit some of his family. He went to the shop of pawnbroker Mr Barras and gave the pawnbroker a ticket for a watch he wanted to redeem. The ticket was found to be the same one that was issued to the man who brought in Broughton's watch on the night of the murder. Smales was promptly handed over to the police.

He was quickly able to produce an alibi proving that he did not commit the murder and told police that he had bought the pawn ticket from 'Charley Normington' for five shillings. The chief constable went over to Whitworth near Castleford on the Sunday morning and managed to trace several witnesses who connected Normington with the ticket. From statements it became clear that on Monday 8 August, two days after the murder of Richard Broughton, two colliers called Jack Fawcett and Henry Batty were in Castleford when they met up with Normington, who knew Fawcett.

The three men went to a pub and once sat down with drinks, Fawcett asked Normington if he would be a hurrier for him at a colliery in Sheffield. Normington agreed and before leaving the pub produced the pawnbroker's ticket offering it to Fawcett. He didn't have enough money to buy it from him, but he took

Normington with him to Jane Dixon's house where he lodged and she agreed to take Normington in for a few days.

Normington continued in his attempts to rid himself of the ticket, offering it to other lodgers before finally selling it to Smales. Meanwhile, Jane Dixon was having doubts about her new lodger. A couple of days after he moved in, she supplied him with a bowl of water which he used to wash a handkerchief. Dixon was alarmed to find the water turn red and when she asked Normington where the blood had come from he took the handkerchief, and, despite it being wet, put it into his waistcoat. When he left the house he left behind a shirt which Dixon suspected of containing spots of blood. The shirt was subsequently given to Mr Nunnely, a surgeon of Leeds, who also had taken possession of the trousers belonging to Bearder.

There was other evidence to incriminate Normington. One witness said that he had seen him and another man about a quarter of a mile from the murder scene on the morning on which the fatal attack had taken place, aadding that Normington had a thick stick or hedgestake with him, which was almost certainly the same weapon which had been found in a field near the site of the murder.

Upon hearing of the concerns of several people who had come into contact with Normington in the days and weeks since the murder, Leeds City Police compiled evidence until they had enough to charge him. Normington was finally arrested in Sheffield where he had been working as a hurrier in a colliery. Chief Constable Stephen English disguised himself as a collier so as not to arouse suspicion. Upon seizing him, English said: 'I apprehend you on the charge of murdering Richard Broughton at Roundhay, near Leeds, on Saturday, the 6th of August.' The nineteen-year-old protested his innocence, saying that he had not been to Leeds for four months and that he had bought the pawn ticket from an Irish man who he met somewhere between Leeds and Wakefield on Sunday, 7 August.

Whilst in custody Normington changed his story and gave the following evidence to Chief Constable English. Normington said:

On Saturday we took a walk up them fields, and there was an oldish man passed by me when I was loosing my breeches, and I was going to do a job for myself; and when I got up, this old man was knocked down, but I never went up to him. I was 50 or 60 yards off when it was done. He got the watch, this young man, whom I lit upon.

In the statement Normington said that the other man had knocked Broughton down with a stick and had then forced him to go into a pawnshop with the watch. He added:

I saw the old man sit down; he had his hat off; I saw him bleeding; he was on the floor, and his head and back was resting against a stoop, and when I saw him bleeding I ran away. I was not against the man when he was knocked down. He had the stick in his hand, and I saw him raising his hand with the stick in it over his shoulder, in the act of striking the old man. I heard the old man screaming and shouting, and I saw the old man down on the floor, and I ran off with my breeches unbuttoned, and that stick which ye had in the court; he had it over his shoulder when I lit on him in Marsh Lane that morning.

After appearing before Leeds magistrates, Normington was committed for trial at the Winter Assizes in York in late December 1859. The *Bradford Observer* noted of Normington:

He is a stiff-set man, bowlegged, and about five feet high, of idle, dissolute habits. He appeared little concerned at his position when under examination, and cross-examined several of the witnesses, for the purpose of getting them to admit that he had said that he had bought the pawn-ticket for the watch. He failed, however, in obtaining any such admission. Normington has confessed that he was one of the men who stopped the deceased, but he denies that he used the bludgeon with which the fatal blows were inflicted.

Many people gave evidence at the trial including Jane Dixon with whom Normington had lodged. Recounting the episode with the handkerchief she said that the stains were of a dark colour, saying that she suspected it to be blood and that she had also seen spots of blood on a shirt that Normington had hung up in his room.

Mr Campbell Foster, representing Normington said that the murder had attracted great attention within the region. He conceded that Normington was in the area where the murder was committed that morning and that he had tried to pawn the watch, but he added that this did not make him guilty of murder.

He said that Normington was simply an accessory to a robbery with violence and a receiver of stolen property, knowing it to be stolen. Therefore, he argued that the jury should find him not guilty of murder, in the knowledge that he would still be punished for the lesser crime.

The jury heard the Judge sum up at length before retiring but they were only out of court for a quarter of an hour before returning with a verdict of 'guilty'. The judge assumed the black cap and pronounced a sentence of death. He said the prisoner had been found guilty of the most horrid of crimes, and 'it appeared that he had never known the deceased before, and to be hanged until he is dead, and may the Lord have mercy on your soul.'

As the sentence of death was passed a piercing shriek rang through the court; it came from the mouth of Normington's mother who was sitting in the side gallery. Normington himself, on being removed from the dock, collapsed into the arms of the under-governor.

After the sentence was passed Normington was unable to walk from the dock across the castle yard and into the condemned cell and when he finally reached his cell he collapsed into floods of tears. Mr Green the deputy governor stressed to Normington the importance of making good use of the short time left to him and not tell any more lies.

Normington replied:

I will not. It was me that did it and the other man stood by. It was me that got his watch. I gave it to him [meaning the other man] *and he kept it while we got to Leeds. I went to pawn it. I have not been in his company before that day. We went that morning near to Marsh Lane railway station and he told me his name and where he lived.* [Normington could not recollect the place but said that a fair was held there.] *We went into a free pawnshop and after we'd pawned the watch I gave him three shillings and kept the other for myself and then we parted.*

During the last week of his life, Normington wrote to his mother:

Dear mother – deeply convinced of the awful in which I am now placed, for in a short time I shall be no more in this world, and I should be very glad to see you before that awful time arrives, as it will be the last opportunity of having an interview with you. From your affectionate son, Charles Normington.

He then got a reply back:

My dear son – I have greatly lamented the condition in which you are placed, but I am glad to hear that you are preparing for another and a better world than this, and I shall be with you on Wednesday next, if all be well, I am almost heart broken when I think of your position, and have prayed for God to have mercy upon you. From your affectionate mother, M Normington.

Mother and son met for the last time in York Castle on the Wednesday before his death. Few prisoners received a death sentence without some attempt by family and friends to try and change the verdict to one of penal servitude for life. However, in this case no effort was made as it was felt that due to the magnitude of the crime, it would be futile to try and organise a

The Debtor's Prison at York Castle, where Charles Normington was executed on New Year's Eve, 1859. York Castle Museum

petition. Normington accepted this and appeared to grow in strength as the execution date approached.

Poorly educated, Normington was unable to write, but he persuaded one of the officers in York Castle to write a letter for him to Chief Constable English.

Dear sir, I now take the opportunity of writing these few lines to you, hoping they will find you in good health. I now beg to tell you that I have had a very fair trial. I can assure you that I am very contented in my mind; and I now tell you that I am happier than I was on the day of the trial, I am prepared for a better place than this. I hope that you will look after that other man. I assure you I have made my peace with God, and I lay all my trust in him; now I think this dreadful crime of which I am convicted was turned to my eternal good. If it had not have happened I should not have gone to the place which I am prepared for; I lay all my trust in the Lord Jesus Christ. I forgive all my enemies, and send my best respects to all inquiring friends.

I hope you will give my best respects to Paddy Byrnes and all his sons and daughters; likewise to John Fawcett and his wife-him that was with me when you took me. I wish you would tell me that I am very comfortable in my mind for I will assure you that I am not frightened of the fate that I am placed before. Yours truly, Charles Normington.

On Saturday, 31 December 1859 at York Castle, Charles Normington was bought onto the scaffold attended by the regular officials.

At St George's Field, opposite the portion of the castle where the scaffold was erected, some people had congregated, anxious to try and obtain a good view of the spectacle. Throughout the morning the number of people increased with arrivals by rail and road, the eventual crowd estimated at between eight and ten thousand.

Normington was pinioned between eleven and twelve o'clock and as the hour of midday struck, he was walked to the scaffold supported by two of the officers and preceded by the chaplain. Though he walked steadily, he looked around anxiously and appeared to have aged during his stay in prison. He was still a teenager but would have passed for a man twice his age. Normington shook hands with the chaplain after the service had

Copy of the 'Full particulars of the trial, confession and execution of Charles Normington'. York Castle Museum

been concluded and then Askern, the executioner, stepped forward.

Normington's legs and arms were pinioned and Askern put the white cap over Normington's head before adjusting the noose. The bolt was immediately withdrawn and the prisoner fell heavily. He was strongly convulsed with his knees up to his body but died within a minute and a half. The body was suspended for the usual amount of time and was then cut down and eventually buried within the precincts of the prison.

In the weeks after the execution, Chief Constable English and other West Riding superintendents received a number of letters from people who claimed to be accomplices of Normington in the murder. The notoriety of the crime led to many people wanting to share in it. However, police took these letters seriously and the senders were soon willing to prove their innocence!

Chapter 12

Murders and Unsolved Mysteries
1865, 1881, 1908

Irish Murder

Patrick Welsh, an Irish labourer aged thirty-three was indicted for having wilfully murdered fellow Irishman John Rouane in Leeds on 29 October 1865. The day before, Saturday, 28 October, Rouane, a bricklayer's labourer and a man called Doherty were together with their wives at a pub called *The Shuttle* in Lower Cross Street. At about midnight, the foursome made their way back towards their homes which were in the same street. The women got home but the two men stopped to chat to a friend who was walking by. While they were talking, Welsh, who also lived in Lower Cross Street, passed the group of men and went to his front door. He shouted that he would fight 'any bloody man'.

Doherty asked him if he had any stones in his pocket to which Welsh answered, 'plenty for thee'. Doherty decided to walk away from a possible fight, but Rouane remained outside. Soon after Doherty opened his door and took his coat off; there was a knock at the door. He was told that his friend had been stabbed. Welsh had thrown out a challenge to fight any man and Rouane replied that he was not frightened and would 'have him'. The two fought until Rouane shouted out, 'I'm done' and fell to the ground. He had been stabbed in the stomach.

An ambulance was called and Rouane was taken to Leeds Infirmary. While in hospital, he was able to make the following declaration:

As God is my judge I am going to die, and believe myself, as far as I can feel, that my last hour is at hand. I was wounded in the belly between 11 and 12 o'clock on Saturday night. I had been at a public house with Patrick Doherty, but I was sober, and so was Doherty. I have known Patrick Welsh four years. We met him in

Leeds General Infirmary. John Rouane was taken here after being stabbed by Patrick Welsh. The author

Lower Cross-street, where he lives as well as I do. He said he would have it out of me, and before I could speak he struck me in the cheek, and made a charge at me, and struck me in the belly. I saw no weapon in his hand when he came up to me, but when he hit me in the belly I put my hand down and felt a knife in his hand.

The wound worsened in hospital due to inflammation of the pericardium and Rouane died on the Monday in hospital.

Welsh tried to get away after the incident, but he was found in Goole the following Monday and was arrested. He told police that he had been provoked into action and said that a cousin of his was playing cards with Rouane and some other friends on the previous Sunday. An argument took place and Rouane and his friends punched and kicked the cousin. Welsh decided to renew the argument on the Saturday morning (the day of the murder). He said that on the Saturday night, before the fatal stabbing took place, he had been punched and kicked by

Rouane, who was being encouraged by his friends to 'kill the bastard'.

An inquest into the death of John Rouane took place at Leeds Town Hall on the Monday morning and he was sent for trial at the Winter Assizes. At the trial, evidence came from a girl called Mary Foody who said that Welsh passed her on the way from his house. She said that he had a knife in his hand and the blade was open. Just before the argument between Welsh and Rouane began, Welsh's wife told him that many people were calling him and he replied: 'Never mind, anyone that faces you shall face me, either David Foody, John Doherty, or Patrick Rounane.' Rouane then said: 'I never was duffer and never shall be one.'

Leeds Town Hall where the inquest into the death of John Rouane took place. The author

The witness saw Welsh and Rouane grappling for about three minutes and then heard Rouane say: 'Loose my trousers for I am done.' Another witness, Bridget Wallace also said that she saw Welsh with the knife.

The jury, after retiring for forty minutes, returned to the court and Patrick Welsh was found guilty of wilful murder. He seemed astonished at the verdict and left his head on the dock rails whilst the judge passed the sentence of death.

The judge said to him:

Patrick Welsh, you have been found guilty of the crime of wilful murder. After a very careful and patient investigation of all the circumstances of your case by the jury. I cannot say that I think they have not come to the right conclusion. It's quite clear that you were, if not quite sober at the time when you killed the deceased, at least you knew well what you were about. You do not appear to have had any quarrel with him at the time, but the jury you see have probably believed, that before you went up to him, you opened your knife with the intention of doing him at least serious bodily harm, if not killing him.

Welsh was visited in the condemned cell by his wife and children. In prison he was generally quiet and well behaved. After a petition was launched on his behalf, he was given a respite by the Home Office upon appeal as the existence of malice aforethought was not legally and fully established. His sentence was, therefore, reduced to penal servitude for life.

Murder in the Inn

The Armley Feast took place in September 1865 and one of the main attractions was the travelling theatre of Mr Wilde. The principal dancer in the theatre was Jane Banham, the tall, attractive twenty-five-year-old wife of an equestrian, who was based in Australia.

After her husband had left her to start a new life on the other side of the world, she began an affair with a man called John Hannah. A tailor, tall and thin in appearance, who lived in Manchester, Hannah was three years her junior. The couple had two children and lived together until Christmas 1864 when she left him after an argument and moved in with her father, John

Hope, who was living in Blackburn. He was leader of the band and a scene painter at the Wilde Theatre.

After Banham left, Hannah made repeated attempts to try and entice her back and he travelled to Armley for the feast when he found out that she would be travelling with the theatre. He made contact and asked her to meet him in the *Malt Hill Inn*; she agreed and went there accompanied by her father and her two children.

In the parlour of the inn, Hannah initially tried once again to get her to return to him but she refused and, sensing an argument, her father took their youngest child out of the room leaving Banham and her eldest child alone with Hannah. After a few minutes screams could be heard coming from the parlour and the first person to open the door to see what was happening was greeted by the sight of Banham on the floor with Hannah leaning over her cutting her throat with a razor. The child was standing by, paralysed with fear and splattered with his mother's blood.

An attempt was made to restrain Hannah and rescue the woman but he continued in a state of frenzy to deepen the wound until he had almost severed the head. The skirt, shawl and bonnet of Banham had been torn off and the floor was saturated with blood. Strewn across the floor was some money which had fallen from the pockets of the murderer or his victim. Those who came into the room were transfixed with horror. Hannah stood up, walked deliberately to the door and then ran off though he was chased and quickly captured before being taken into custody in Leeds.

An inquest was held the following morning at the *Malt Hill Inn* in the room above the parlour where the murder had taken place. There was great excitement as word spread of the horrors of the previous night and there were screams of protest when two wardens brought Hannah back to the inn from the prison.

The scene of the murder was visited by many people in the days following the murder with visitors from Leeds, Bradford, Dewsbury, Huddersfield and other towns, having read about the murder in the local papers, now wanting to see exactly where it had taken place. The landlord of the pub saw the crowds of visitors as a way of bringing in much needed custom and the stains of blood on the matting and the paper on the walls of the room were not removed. Visitors to the *Malt Hill Inn* were shown evidence of the struggle, which had taken place, and people had torn bits of paper off the walls to take as mementoes.

Hannah was committed for trial at the Winter Assizes and pleaded to the jury. 'All I want is for them to consider and give me justice.' He wept loudly as most of the evidence was given, but the jury took just a quarter of an hour before returning to court to judge him guilty of murder. Hannah fainted and had to be taken out of court unconscious before being sent to York Castle and placed in the condemned cell. He admitted his guilt and said he would feel better about going to heaven if Banham was there to greet him.

While in prison he said that he did not go to Armley with the intention of harming Jane Banham but admitted that he had been drinking heavily before they met. They had a violent argument which ended with him hitting her. She provoked him further by showing him an image of another man she claimed she had been seeing. Hannah said that he then got out a razor with the intention of frightening her, but it didn't work and they fought with each other. He then said that he cut his hands and 'maddened by drink and upset at being scorned' he made a dash for her, cutting her throat with the razor.

A Murder Waiting to Happen

Sarah Whittaker, a neighbour of Thomas Mead and Clara Howell said that she thought there would be a murder in their household and she was to prove a good judge of character.

Clara Howell, thirty-eight, and Thomas Mead, a gasworker, five years her junior, lived together at Crooks Yard, West Street. Throughout the seven years they had been together, their neighbourhood had more than once reverberated to the sound of a violent row coming from the house. The people of Crooks Yard heard more shouts and screams on the night of Friday, 27 November 1908 and the situation became so bad the police were finally called to the house. However, after they left, at about one in the morning the noise began again and continued for two hours. Nothing more was heard from the house and Mead left home at nine o'clock the next morning.

He passed Sarah Whittaker who was washing her front step and asked her what she thought about their situation. She replied, 'What do I think of you both? If there's not an altercation soon, there'll be murder.' Mead added: 'There will an' all.' Sarah asked where Clara was and Mead told her that she had gone to stay with her mother.

It was unlike Clara to stay away from the house too long and as the day passed, Sarah became concerned. Finally, the next morning, she contacted the police and constable F W Barbutt went with her to the house. Finding it locked he decided to climb up to the bedroom window.

He smashed the pane with his truncheon and climbed in to find the body of Clara Howell in the corner of the room hidden underneath a pile of rags. Her body was covered in bruises and the constable believed she had been kicked to death.

After leaving his house Mead had gone to a pub for a drink. He began talking to a man called John William Prenderville and freely confessed that he had killed Clara. He told Prenderville that she had taken some money out of his pocket and that he had struck her. She fell over and he had carried her to bed where she died after a few minutes.

Later in the pub he spoke to some other drinkers and, with the alcohol beginning to talk, he became involved in a fight. The landlord threw him out onto the street and Mead shouted back at him: 'I have done one in, let me go back and chivy him, if you don't believe me take the key and go look.' Later that night Mead appeared on the doorstep of number five, Lisbon Court, which was owned by Mick Robinson, a friend of his. Robinson's daughter Margaret Shuttleworth was staying there and she let him sleep on the sofa.

She asked about Clara but Mead said that if Robinson knew what he had done, he would not let him stay there. He confessed to Shuttleworth that he had given Clara two black eyes and killed her. Initially she didn't believe Mead but a neighbour later came to the house and breathlessly told Shuttleworth that Clara Howell had been found dead by the police. Mead took this as his cue to leave and he quickly grabbed his cap and ran off.

He went to the house of another friend, this time in Chadwick Place and it was here, on the Monday night, that Mead was arrested. He was taken to New Wortley police station and said to the arresting officers: 'She is dead, as dead as a mackerel. If you had been an hour later, I should have done myself in.'

As he was placed in a cell, Mead spoke to constable Wright, asking if he had seen the body. He added:

> Well I have done it. I shall have to swing for her. She made me do it. I woke on Saturday morning. She had taken all my money. We then got on about it. I gave her a good hiding. I hope to God they will hang me. I didn't want to live. How long shall I have to wait?

Mead was committed for trial in Leeds on 10 February 1909. It emerged that the couple lived in poor conditions with the living room in a particular state. The only furniture in the room was a wooden chair and that had been smashed to pieces during the night the murder took place. Bloodstains had indicated that Clara Howell had been attacked downstairs and then stripped of her clothing and carried upstairs. The court heard that Clara was often seen with black eyes and bruises and that when she was found she was bruised from head to toe. She also had cuts on her head, a black eye and a broken nose. A broken broom handle was found near to the body covered in bloodstains.

The defence counsel attempted to argue that the jury should return a verdict of manslaughter, as Mead was so drunk at the time of the attack that he did not know what he was doing. However, after a short consideration, the jury ignored this advice and returned a guilty verdict. Mead was duly sentenced to death.

The execution of Thomas Mead was set for Friday, 12 March 1909. Appeals took place against the sentence but they were dismissed and Mead became resigned to his fate. He was quiet during his first few days in the condemned cell at Armley Gaol and did not talk about the murder; however, he appeared to improve and began talking to other prisoners and warders though he still refused to talk about Clara Howell.

On his last morning he ate a hearty breakfast and prepared himself to be pinioned by the executioners. Officials were said to be taken aback at the calm way in which he went to his death. He did not speak on the scaffold and his death was instantaneous. A number of women and children gathered at the lower end of the street leading to the jail but they dispersed when the tolling of the bell gave the news that Mead had been executed.

Batley Mystery

At half-past four on the morning of 30 May 1881, a miner called Peter Kelley and his young son were walking down Batley High Street on their way to the West End Colliery in the town. The boy noticed what he thought was a sack on the doorstep of a butchers shop which belonged to Mary Wigglesworth. His father, on closer examination, found that it contained the body of a man, half-reclining on the door, half-lying on the doorstep.

Kelley immediately went to report the matter at Batley Police Station and sergeants Addy and Marshall carried the body over to the *Victoria Hotel* in the town. They soon established that the body was that of John Critchley, the son of James Critchley, JP of Batley Hall and brother of Robert Critchley, a West Riding magistrate.

Police who investigated the scene of the discovery saw no evidence that Critchley had been murdered, however there were some circumstances which led police to believe that the man had been the victim of 'brutal violence' which may have been the cause of death.

The man was naked apart from a pair of trousers and a hat when he was found. A coat and vest, believed to belong to Critchley were discovered on the doorstep. The hands were crossed over the chest and the wrists were tightly tied together with a piece of cord. Critchley's feet were also tied together with a piece of rope. The head, neck, chest and other parts of the body were found to be very swollen, but there were relatively few marks on the body, so the swelling may have been caused by internal problems rather than any violence.

Decomposition had set in, and it was established that the man had been dead for over twenty-four hours. However, the body had not been in the place it was found for very long. The policeman, whose beat included the High Street, confirmed that he had passed the shop at about half-past two in the morning and he had seen nothing on the doorstep at that time.

Despite being born into an illustrious family, John Critchley,

A modern view of part of Batley town centre. The author

who was unmarried, had lived an unconventional life. For several months he had visited home very rarely and was not often seen in the Batley area. He was most often found in Bradford and Leeds, especially a well-known temperance hotel when in Bradford. Miss Wigglesworth, who owned the butchers shop said that she knew the deceased man, indeed the two had been having a relationship, but had not seen him for some time and knew little of where he had been in the weeks prior to his death.

In the days that followed the discovery of the body, rumours circulated as to why the body should have been disposed of in that place in particular; the doorstep of the shop owned by Critchley's former lover. One theory was that the body had been carried to its resting place by people who knew of the relationship between Critchley and Wigglesworth and left it there because of a grudge against the woman or merely to baffle police; something they succeeded in doing! The police were also confused on the cause of death. Had he died of natural causes or been killed? If he had died of natural causes, why was the body found on the doorstep of the shop belonging to Mary Wigglesworth?

The bare facts pointed to a murder and the body having been dumped on the shop doorway. The two most popular theories doing the rounds at Batley police station were, firstly, that he had been murdered somewhere outside of Batley and the body had been dumped onto the doorstep, or he had died suddenly, in circumstances embarrassing to himself or people around him. Therefore, either out of consideration to his family and friends, or to avoid suspicion, whoever was with Critchley when he died, decided to get rid of the body and left it where it was eventually found.

In Critchley's pockets were found an empty purse, a knife, some letters and other papers and several photographs including one of Mary Wigglesworth. There were also a number of pawn tickets, which were investigated by police who were hoping to get some clues as to where the man had been in recent weeks and how he had been spending his time.

The police had found the case difficult to solve, not least because Critchley was not in any particular job at the time of his death; he moved around frequently so was not tied to one place with one set of people who could vouch for his movements over the weeks prior to his death. The police were further hindered by the fact that his friends were slow to come forward, perhaps given the suspicious nature of his death. They were seemingly anxious to avoid any connection with the death in any way.

The *Yorkshire Post* gave its assumption:

The supposition which we ventured to hazard yesterday, that the unhappy man had probably died amongst the companions of his wretchedness, and that they, to clear themselves of possible odium, got rid of the body in the most ingenious manner they could hit upon, seems to be regarded as the most probable theory.

The inquest into the death of John Critchley opened at the *Victoria Hotel* some sixteen hours after the body had first been discovered. Large numbers of people had assembled outside the hotel as the death had attracted a great deal of local interest with many theories put forward on how Critchley had met his end. Due to the vast numbers of people attracted by this case, the examination took place at half-past four in the morning.

Among those giving evidence was Walter Critchley, John's younger brother who said that John was forty-three-years-old and did not have a job at the time of his death. When he was in business, he had been a card maker.

Victoria Hotel *in Batley.* The author

The inquest heard that the appearance of Critchley's head on the day he was found suggested that the body might have been immersed in water for several days. This theory gained further ground due to the discolouration, swelling and decomposition of the body. However, another, perhaps more likely explanation for the state of the body was the, as the papers described it, dissipation, which Critchley had enjoyed over a period of time.

The contents of the stomach were analysed so as to determine whether poison had been administered in any form. Mr Thomas Scattergood, the surgeon who performed the post-mortem, told the inquest that he had analysed the stomach and found it contained about two fluid ounces of partially digested food, with the only recognisable elements being fat and starch.

He also reported that the colon had patches of redness, apparently due to slight inflammation, but this was not sufficient to cause death. However, the heart was in a state of fatty degeneration and the liver was also diseased through increased fat. The gall bladder was full of small calculi. Based upon these results, Scattergood said he believed that there was no ground for supposing that the deceased man died from poisoning.

The substance of what the inquest had heard was that Critchley was seen on 26 May in the 'refreshment rooms' of one of the witnesses in Bradford and that he was found on the doorstep of the shop four days later. Death, it had been established, must have been at least forty-eight hours before the discovery of the body, which may well have been the reason why there was a gap between Thursday afternoon and Friday midnight when the police had no clue or trace of the man's whereabouts.

The coroner said that every opportunity had been given to people who wanted to give evidence and that if the jury were satisfied that the death was the result of natural causes, they should return a verdict to that effect. As the medical testimony was satisfactory and there were no marks of violence on the body, and there was no evidence of poisoning, the coroner said he did not see that they could go any further.

The jury deliberated, for about a quarter of an hour, after which it became clear that some were in doubt regarding the evidence given by Dr O'Reilly who made the post-mortem examination. He believed that the man died from natural causes, but that was challenged by several of the jurors. The coroner asked him if it was possible that Critchley could have been strangled, but the doctor said no and said it was his belief that fatty degeneration of the heart was the cause of death.

The jury, once again left to consider the matter. When they returned after about twenty minutes, they gave the following verdict:

> *That John Critchley was found dead on a doorstep in Carlinghow on the 30th May 1881, and the jury are unanimous in their verdict, based on medical evidence, that the deceased died from natural causes.*

The foreman of the jury went on to say that, although the jury was satisfied with the verdict, questions remained as to where the body was found and how it came to be there. He expressed

Batley churchyard. The author

a hope that police would 'use every endeavour' to ascertain how the body of Critchley came to be on the doorstep of the butchers shop on that morning. Even if Critchley was not killed, it is likely that he died in 'unfortunate circumstances' and the people with him wanted to dispose of the body, hence leaving it where they knew it would be found. However, nobody came forward and the mystery remained.

Chapter 13

Suicides
1849-1909

The subject of suicide is a difficult subject even today, but in Victorian times it was often felt too awful to discuss. Only the suicides of men such as 'the fallen favourite or functionary' who had risen above his station and then encountered sudden disgrace, were likely to be reported.

Up until 1961 suicide was a crime, so the knowledge that the dead person had broken the law was added to the personal tragedy involved. To go back before the Victorian era can be found a very different attitude to suicide, reflected in what happened at the coroners' inquests into particular cases.

Coroners are first mentioned in 1194. The coroner's role in investigating deaths was important because it could lead to the seizure of property, as the Crown could take the possessions of a murderer. People who had taken their own lives were seen as self-murderers, so, as with other murderers, their property was forfeit to the Crown. However, those who were seen as 'mad' could not be held responsible for their actions so this did not involve forfeiture and they were allowed a Christian burial. The distinction between whether a suicide was sane or not was thus very important both to the Crown and to the family of the deceased.

Under Henry VIII, Protestant religious fervour brought the conviction that suicides had given in to the Devil and were therefore, particularly sinful. This attitude lasted until the end of the seventeenth century when there was a shift in belief to a more sympathetic view. Coroners started to become less conscientious about passing their papers on to the assize judges. Frequently, they simply submitted a list of the inquests they conducted to the Quarter Sessions so they could be paid for their work. These records usually contain the verdicts.

It was not just in England that suicide was regarded as an unspeakable crime. A French law of 1670 required the body of a suicide to be dragged through the streets, before it was thrown into a sewer or on the town dump. In 1660, Massachusetts passed a law that the body of a suicide victim was to be buried at the crossroads of a highway. One pagan belief was that the soul of a suicide was bound to wander; that was less likely to happen, however, if the body was buried at a crossroads with a stake through the heart.

The tolerance towards suicides that juries showed lasted into the early-nineteenth century, but the Victorian religious revival brought an increasingly harsh attitude. Verdicts of *felo de se* became more common and it was not until 1870 that forfeiture of suicides' property ceased, although by that time the Crown rarely exercised its rights, unless another crime was involved.

The burial of suicide victims was also different from those of deaths from natural causes. An Act of 1823 had put an end to the practice of burying victims in some public highway with a stake driven through them but as late as 1882, by law, a suicide victim had to be buried at night. Eventually, suicide victims were given permission to be buried in churchyards, but between the hours of 9 pm and midnight, and without the rites of the church.

John Marks

In Leeds, John Marks killed himself in what was described as a distressing suicide. Marks sold chemical preparations from which he made a living, however, he was struggling to make ends meet. He lodged in Skinner Lane with a couple called Oliver and, Mrs Oliver said that since Christmas 1880, Marks had been very depressed. When asked how he was, Marks told her: 'Oh, I am bothered to pieces.' He told her he was troubled about a society with which he was connected and that he was about to be excluded from it. It was later learnt that he was a freemason.

On a Monday afternoon in June 1881, Mrs Oliver went to the door to Marks's room but found it locked. She heard moaning coming from the room and asked her son to fetch a ladder and climb in through the window. There he found Marks unconscious and despite receiving medical help, Marks died as a result of narcotic poisoning. A jug labelled 'morphia' and which had recently been used, was discovered near his bed.

Under his pillow was found a note which read:

In leaving I only hope that more mercy may be extended to you than you have granted to me. To those belonging to me I have no means of making reparation, and consequently must be dumb because overwhelmed.

Barker Tragedy

Fred Barker, aged thirty, attacked his mother and brothers before committing suicide in a horrific attack in March 1909.

Mrs Barker, a widow, lived with her five children in a small two-bedroomed house in Woolwich Street, Holbeck. She had a hard struggle to bring the boys up, especially as two were disabled and in the previous few months the family had been entirely dependent upon the incomes of the two elder sons Albert and Fred. However, Albert got married and left home leaving Fred as the only source of income.

Fred was worried at this responsibility, though he did not share his concerns with his mother or Albert. He earnt a decent living as a moulder having completed his apprenticeship in the trade, but he still felt that there was insufficient money there on which to feed and clothe the entire family.

He became especially depressed over the weekend of Albert's wedding and on the Monday he came in from work feeling ill. He rested until about five-thirty when his mother woke him to get him ready to go back to work.

However, weeks of worry regarding his and the family's future came to a terrifying conclusion and Barker appeared downstairs wielding a hatchet, aiming a blow at his mother's head. She screamed out but was unable to defend herself and blows continued to rein down onto her head until she fell to the ground unconscious. Fred's brother Herbert, who was disabled, was in a bed downstairs and was also attacked, left bleeding profusely from cuts on the forehead.

Fred then went upstairs where his brother Billy had been woken by the screaming in the house. He saw his brother come into his room carrying a hatchet and began to scream. Also disabled, he was powerless to protect himself and after a blow from the hatchet, he was also left unconscious on his bed.

The youngest brother Walter, in a state of terror, sat down near the foot of his bed and pulled the sheets over his head, but he was left untouched. Fred Barker then went back upstairs and cut his throat. Neighbours were soon on the scene. They had been alerted by screams and shouts coming from the house and one of the first people to get into the house was Dr Ladell who found the mother sitting in a chair, bathed in blood.

Albert was told of the attack by neighbours and hurried to the house to find his mother unconscious, with her head and face covered in blood. He also found Herbert and Billy on their beds bleeding with cuts to their faces, before going up the stairs and finding his brother Fred, lying dead in a bedroom. Albert was shocked and said that prior to the attack, the family had been living happily with no clue of the horror to come.

Fred was described as being industrious and respectable; he was also a teetotaller and non-smoker. He gave his wages to his mother with whom he had a good relationship, so the attack came as a great shock to neighbours of the family.

Critically injured in the attack by her son, Mrs Barker died two days later. The two brothers suffered fractured skulls but recovered; though they were rocked by the tragic news of their mother and big brother.

Edward Askin

Edward Askin, aged just fifteen killed himself after a family argument in December 1859. Askin lived with his parents in Charley Street, New Road End and already had a reputation as a very intense teenager. He told his parents that he wanted to keep some hens in the house, but his mother refused, saying that they would become a nuisance in the neighbourhood and she advised him to place the money he would have spent on buying the hens into a savings account.

He resented the advice and pulled off his coat and waistcoat before throwing them into the fire. His mother retrieved them as quickly as she could but they were ruined.

He appeared to calm down after this outburst and went out, returning at about ten o'clock on the Saturday night. The following morning he returned to the topic of keeping hens and she partially relented, promising to allow him to save a shilling a week out of his earnings to place in the savings bank. She said that when he had saved up enough money, they would talk again about the possibility of him buying hens. Again he appeared to

Charley Street, where Edward Askin lived. Leeds Library and Information Services

Leeds Town Hall, where the inquest into the death of Edward Askin was held. The author

be satisfied but, testimony to his intense personality, he later refused to get out of his bed and have his breakfast. He also began singing very loudly. His father called out for him to stop and he went quieter, eventually stopping altogether.

His parents assumed he had gone back to sleep and he was allowed to remain undisturbed, but about midday his father went up to wake him up and discovered his son suspended from the bed. He managed to get Edward down, but he was already dead.

The following Monday at the Leeds Town Hall, Edward Blackburn, the coroner held an inquest which heard that three months ago Askin had twice tried to hang himself but was cut down on each occasion by his mother and another time he had threatened to stab her. The jury, having heard the evidence, gave a verdict of suicide caused by temporary insanity.

Matthew Atkin

In February 1868 the body of a man called Matthew Atkin, aged fifty-nine, was found dead in Haymount Street, Newtown. The dead man was a tailor, who was married but had become ill and had recently gone blind. The loss of his sight had led to deep depression and on a Wednesday night he had gone to bed as usual but on waking at about four in the morning his wife was surprised to discover that he was not in the room with her.

She eventually found him lying in the cellar with a deep gash to his throat. The jugular vein was severed and despite frantic efforts, he soon died. The subsequent inquest decided that he had committed suicide whilst temporarily insane.

Elizabeth Goy

A case of *felo de se* occurred in St Peter's Square, St Peter's Street, Leeds involving Elizabeth Goy. Goy, who was aged twenty-four was originally from Hull where she married a sailor. However, she left him and moved to Leeds where she set up home with another man called Edward Brown, a fish hawker and a fiddler. He left their house at seven on a Wednesday morning in June 1849 and did not return home until one o'clock the next morning.

On entering the house, Brown found Goy very ill in bed, suffering from violent sickness. She refused to tell him the cause of it until

St Peter's Square. The author

about half an hour later when she admitted that she had taken poison. Her condition deteriorated and she died the same day.

At the Coroner's Inquest held in the court-house the next day, it was stated by a woman who lived next door that she had accompanied Goy to a druggist the previous day at the end of Corn Hill. Goy bought and took home a pennyworth of Arsenic. She said that she wanted to buy it to kill black beetles which swarmed in the house. However, she also noticed that Goy was depressed about her health and she had doubts in her mind when she saw Goy so determined to buy the Arsenic.

The neighbour did not leave Goy until ten o'clock at night when she appeared to be feeling a little better and there was nothing suspicious about her behaviour.

The jury under the circumstances felt justified in returning a verdict of *felo de se*. Testimony to the shame in which suicide was felt in the nineteenth century, the remains of Goy were buried in the Burmantofts cemetery between eleven and twelve on the Thursday night without any religious ceremony.

James Foreman

The residents of Richmond Hill were startled when they heard the news that a man called James Foreman living in Sussex Street had committed suicide in June 1856. A wood carver aged fifty-seven and a widower, Foreman had, for some time, held the post of secretary to a friendly society and about a month before his suicide he became worried that his accounts for the society were incorrect.

This preyed upon his mind and he sank into a deep depression. He made an attempt to cut his throat but was discovered in time to save his life, but was closely watched from now on by family and friends, though his depression appeared to worsen in the days just before his death.

One morning, despite the attentions of his friends, he managed to get possession of a razor and whilst alone for a few minutes he managed to cut his throat. On entering the bedroom, his friends saw Foreman kneeling on the floor with his throat cut from ear to ear. His head was above a basin which was half-filled with blood. He was still alive when people came to his aid but died a couple of minutes later. The inquest recorded the expected verdict of suicide.

Monkbridge. The body of James Smith was found near here. Leeds Library and Information Services

James Smith

The body of a man in a state of decomposition was found in the canal near to Monkbridge during April 1866. It was taken to the *Wellington Inn* in Wellington Street, where it lay for identification and eventually the man was identified as James Smith, aged thirty-five.

A man unable to hold onto a job, or onto his money, he lived in Barrack Street, Chapeltown and had been missing for a fortnight before his body was discovered. At the inquest there was no evidence to show how he came to be in the water. However, his pockets were full of stones so it was either his intention to throw himself in or somebody else wanted rid of Smith and put the stones in his pocket to ensure that he drowned.

The jury heard evidence that Smith was virtually destitute and that he had been heard to say to people that he wanted to throw himself in the water. The jury, therefore, returned a verdict of 'drowned'.

Old Leeds Bridge. The Thoresby Society

Samuel Birchall

Samuel Birchall, an engine driver with the Midland Railway Company, committed suicide by poisoning himself with opium. He was fifty-five and had been employed by the company for about twenty years. In addition to his job as an engine driver, he had a small shop in Cross Alfred Street but for the last two years he had been living and working in Sheffield and visiting his family in Leeds every few weeks.

He had been addicted to horse racing for most of his adult life and was described as 'a man of very dissipated habits' and on several occasions he had narrowly escaped dismissal by the company. During June 1866 he spent a weekend with his family back in Leeds. He was drunk throughout the Saturday and Sunday and remarked to his married daughter that he was tired with the world and that he would cause himself harm. He had made similar threats in the past, so his daughter was not unduly worried.

However, before he was due to return to Sheffield he was taken ill whilst with friends. They saw him deteriorate before their eyes and it became clear to them that he had carried out his threat to take opium. As his friends tried to save his life he shouted that all the doctors in the world could do nothing for him and he swore and hit out at his friends.

A stomach pump was applied but the poison in his body had already done too much damage and he died at six in the evening. The two doctors who had been called for by his friends carried out a post-mortem examination and confirmed that death had resulted from a large dose of opium.

At the inquest, several witnesses gave evidence and spoke of his determination to end his life. The jury returned a verdict of *felo de se*.

Select Bibliography

Anning, Stephen T, *History of the Leeds School of Medicine*, 1982.
Anning, Stephen T, *The History of Medicine in Leeds*, 1980.
Barnard, Sylvia M, *Viewing the breathless corpse: coroners and inquests in Victorian Leeds*, 2001.
Briggs, Asa, *Victorian Cities*, 1968.
Burt, Stephen, *Criminal Leeds*, 1980 (?).
Eddleston, John J, *Murderous Leeds*, 1997.
Stevenson-Tate, Lynne, (Ed) *Aspects of Leeds 2*, 1999.
Thornton, David, *Leeds – the story of a city*, 2002.

Index